RALPH WALDO EMERSON

Ralph Waldo Emerson

A PROFILE

EDITED BY

CARL BODE

AMERICAN PROFILES

General Editor: Aïda DiPace Donald

American Century Series

HILL AND WANG : NEW YORK

Contents

Emerson: Enough of His Life to Suggest His Character

Emerson once complained that for forty years his acquaintances greeted him by announcing that he looked thinner than when they had seen him before. I do not want to belabor a symbol and yet there is a certain metaphysical truth to the tactless comment his compeers made. There was always the appearance of a certain bloodlessness about him. He looked not only lean but spiritual. He himself, while denying that he became thinner every day, admitted that he lacked warmth. He was no substitute, he said apologetically, for the kitchen stove. He knew that this was true for his general relationships and true as well for his intimate ones—even, with a single exception, his most intimate ones.

The exception involved Ellen Tucker, whom he married in 1829 when he was twenty-six and she was seventeen. "Oh Ellen, I do dearly love you," he wrote in his journal and there is every evidence that he meant it. However, she died two years later; and we get the impression that for the rest of his long life no one touched him as closely—not even his second wife, Lydian, whom he called "mine Asia"; not even Waldo, his son, who died at the age of five. For we find him writing about the child, not long afterward, that his death was a grievous blow but that it could be borne and in fact in the long run counted for little. This did not mean that Emerson was hard-hearted. It meant that he created a kind of spiritual relation with the world that made matter count for little, even when it was beloved human flesh. Or not count for little—that is unfair —but count for less than it does for most people.

Today a distinguished group of scholars is editing Emerson's *Journals and Miscellaneous Notebooks,* and as they come out, volume after volume, a more humane Emerson is revealed to us. But he is still a man of mind, essentially, more than matter. He is still a great intuitive philosopher, and a great gnomic writer.

The first of these new volumes was published in 1960. When the last will be published no one can tell. But as they appear in imposing procession we see more of Emerson's inner life than we ever have before. The outer life is often important too; but for a writer as remarkably spiritual as Emerson, the weather within is vital to watch. Doubtless the best thing is to strike a balance. The *Journals* themselves help us to do this, for in their pages Emerson writes both of outer and inner events. He records what he reads and reflects on; he records as well, from time to time, what is happening to him and the world around him.

The new set of volumes starts with 1819. The information we have about the years before that can be set down succinctly. Emerson was born May 25, 1803, in Boston. His father, William Emerson, was a prominent Boston minister who, when Ralph arrived, was feeling his way from Congregationalism to the new Unitarianism. In time his son would move still further, from Unitarianism to transcendentalism. A good index to William Emerson's standing was that on the day of his son's birth he dined with the Governor of the state. Ralph's childhood seems to have been usual for those rather precarious days. One of his four brothers died very young, so he saw death early. Not long afterward William Emerson suffered from a lung complaint serious enough to persuade him to move from Boston with its chill sea air to the inland town of Concord, where he had been born. In hard fact there was not much more blandness to Concord's air, but the notion of returning to his native village decided him. The villagers there combined with some of the Boston parishioners William Emerson brought with him to provide a new church, a new parsonage, and some money for the purchase of furniture.

Ralph's childhood days in Concord were passed in the midst of a pious, busy family. He relished some of the family rituals and later perpetuated them. As a middle-aged man he would still order duck turnover served on Thanksgiving because that was what they served when he was a boy.

He respected his father the more because William Emerson was not only a minister but a writer and civic leader. Though Ralph was only eight when his father died, he realized the importance of his father's varied roles. But for all of William Emerson's prominence, the family had a hard time after his death. If they were not exposed to genteel poverty, they were exposed to the next thing above it. Notwithstanding, they managed to send Ralph to the Boston Latin School and supplemented that rather sparse education with other instruction. As important to his education as anything was the arrival of his formidable aunt, Mary Moody Emerson, to help with the household. With her encouragement added to that of others, he started to fulfill the stereotype of the gifted student. He became less boyish and more learned; he began to enjoy writing verse and prose both.

When he was only fourteen he passed the necessary examinations for Harvard and entered as a freshman in 1817. A scholarship boy, he studied and wrote more, and relaxed less, than most of his classmates. He won a prize or two for his writing and also began to do well in public speaking, winning a minor award for it. When he was only seventeen he began keeping his journal and would continue to keep it as long as he could write. He made the first entry early in 1820. From the notes he wrote down and the excerpts entered from his reading we can see the beginning of some of his long-run enthusiasms for classic literature and moral philosophy. At graduation in 1821 he won a prize for an essay on ethical philosophy and became the class poet. However, as a scholar he never achieved anything but a mediocre standing in his class.

Looked at from without, his college career failed to show much distinction. Neither did the teaching, at his brother William's school, which he undertook after graduation. He was writing, however, much of the time. And what he was writing—and thinking—we can see with considerable clarity as the newly edited, complete volumes of his *Journals* are issued.

Although the effect is still that of a Concord saint, from the very first volume we at least see proof that Emerson lived and breathed, that he could be angered or irritated, that he could enjoy the body as well as the mind. He could say "pish" to his occasional pomposity and put it down in the journal. He could make sharp comments about his acquaintances. He could even tell a story about a dancing girl. All this is useful for us to know because it shows that his great goodness was tougher and shrewder than we had suspected. We begin to see more of the connections that his ideas had with earth. The second volume, covering the years from 1822 to 1826, opens with Emerson now nineteen and a Harvard graduate. He faces the problem of making a living. His immediate if uneasy solution is to teach school. He manages to do this, but with only half a mind; and it becomes clear that he is moving toward a career in the ministry. Meanwhile, he writes more.

As he writes, he changes. He still retains the ambitious title he gave his first notebooks, "Wide World," and they are still dedicated to an ideal aim as they were in his Harvard College days. But they show that some of his young optimism is being dissipated. Life is not exactly what he thought and he considers himself ill equipped to deal with it. He sets down his self-accusations, among them: "I am a lover of indolence, & of the belly." And sadly, "What is called a warm heart, I have not." Then the running title "Wide World" disappears and the notebooks are merely numbered. But Emerson's general approach remains the same. He reads omnivorously, copying out the most attractive passages from what he reads. Then he digests them and thereafter sets down his reflections about them. Moral problems are already his chief interest, as they will continue to be throughout his life. He prepares embryo essays on, among other subjects, sympathy, human nature, and providence. He keeps on composing poetry, or rather verse: the poetry will come afterward.

By 1826 he has grown perceptibly. He has nearly lost his eyesight, a dire threat indeed, but an operation restores it. He supplements his teaching with studies at the Harvard Divinity School. This is the time when he falls in love with Ellen Tucker, exclaiming in blank verse, "I am enamoured of thy loveliness." During this single period at any rate, he has no doubt about the warmth of his nature. Though there is no necessary connection, his writing grows better. In his prose the striking, felicitous images that we now associate with him appear increasingly. He is still far from the great poet-prophet of his later years but the promise is there.

In 1826 he begins his career as a Unitarian minister. He quickly achieves a reputation as a spiritual leader of superior mental and moral strength. He receives many invitations to preach and refuses several permanent posts until the right opening is offered. It is the junior pastorship of Boston's famous Second Church. His reputation spreads. He is chosen chaplain of the Massachusetts State Senate; he is elected to the Boston School Committee.

His personal life flowers even more richly than his professional one. Winning Ellen Tucker and marrying her in September, 1829, he enjoys what promises to be an idyllic marriage. But the flowering is brief; she dies after a year and a half, in the conviction that she is going to God. This belief we see Emerson trying his utmost to share, yet his sorrow is too great. He tries the consolation of religion. He tries to lose himself in his writing. The writing is heavy, however, and the consolations of religion are tenuous. In fact Ellen's death arouses religious doubts in him that time will never allay. Such orthodoxy as he has disappears. Gradually he will conceive of an Over-Soul, bland, benevolent, and ethereal, in the place of the deity he first worshiped; but this process will take some years.

By the early 1830's a basic attitude toward life has been formed. In September, 1832, Emerson resigns his pastorate and preaches his farewell sermon. His announced reason is that he can no longer believe in celebrating communion. Then he goes through a period of sickness and uncertainty, which ends by his embarking on a European tour of ten months. He meets great men, including Carlyle, Wordsworth, Coleridge, and Landor. He sees both their strengths and weaknesses. He enjoys the British but becomes no lisping Anglophile. He is candid about places as well as persons, saying about London for example, "Immense city. Very dull city."

On his return he finds it hard to search out a new career. But the times are on his side. Lyceum lecturing, which pays fairly well, has become a vogue, and he drifts into a half-career as a lecturer, drawing on some of the same qualities which had won him prompt recognition in the pulpit. The audiences believe they want education though they as often want entertainment. Yet Emerson, being Emerson, makes a minimum of compromises. Once or twice he scolds himself, "Do, dear, when you come to write Lyceum lectures, remember that you are not to say, What must be said in a Lyceum?" Not incidentally, the Lyceum lectures he writes will become, after many readings to many audiences, the essays on which his fame will rest.

The middle 1830's bring better days for him. The grief over the death of his first wife largely allayed, he marries Lydian Jackson—pale, dark, and serene—and brings her to Concord to preside over his household. He writes the first of the essays which will give him his permanent place in American letters. He calls publicly for a true American literature and, half knowingly, provides part of it himself. He publishes the little book *Nature* in 1836; it will be called the Bible of New England transcendentalism. He writes and delivers "The American Scholar" and the Divinity School Address. The first will become America's literary Declaration of Independence; the second to his amazement will become a success of scandal and will result in Harvard's barring him, in effect, from its public platforms for the next twenty-five years. But elsewhere the platforms of the nation open up to him as his standing as a lecturer rises.

His interests expand, his relationships multiply. In the fall of 1837 he meets Henry Thoreau (if he has not met him before) when Thoreau returns to settle in Concord after graduating from Harvard College. The two diverse men find unexpected affinities. Friendships develop too with Bronson Alcott, the most transcendental of the emerging transcendentalists, and that classic bluestocking, Margaret Fuller. Emerson grows and grasps for new experience. In April, 1838, for instance, he goes to some cliffs with Thoreau and is awed by the prospect. Back home that night, he walks out in the dark and sees only a star and hears only a frog. He asks himself promptly, "Well do not these suffice?" The answer is, They do, and there is no need for a new Niagara each day to hanker after. He learns that less is more.

As his character becomes richer, his observation becomes more penetrating. He is by no means sinking into a state of vegetable benevolence; quite the reverse. He looks wisely about him, scanning and remembering. The result is sometimes quite formidable, as for example, when he is meditating on the Southern character. Emerson recalls his Cambridge days as well as his later experiences, and the observation in his journal is barbed: "The young Southerner comes here a spoiled child with graceful manners, excellent self command, very good to be spoiled more, but good for nothing else, a mere parader. He has conversed so much with rifles, horses, & dogs that he is become himself a rifle, a horse, & a dog and in civil educated company where anything human is going forward he is dumb & unhappy; like an Indian in a church." Emerson adds, "Their question respecting any man is like a Seminole's, How can he fight? In this country, we ask, What can he do?"

By the beginning of the 1840's Emerson is set in the mold he will occupy for the rest of his long life. His first series of essays is published in 1841, his second in 1844. Together they make his reputation as a writer. They reveal an intuitive, unsystematic philosopher and preacher but one with an almost sublime confidence in a few prime principles. He believes in self-reliance, which is also reliance on the Over-Soul. He believes in a cosmos founded on moral and Platonic ideas. To simplify his transcendentalism, we can say that he believes that mind transcends matter (though both exist) and intuition transcends tuition (though both operate).

He concerns himself little with particulars and much with generalities. He characteristically takes the long view. This is one of the reasons for his seeming bloodless at times, not only to others but to himself. Even a death does not long jar his composure. He goes on writing and lecturing, addressing himself to the cosmos as usual. One after another his books come out; they deepen and widen his reputation. Gradually he becomes known as one of his nation's most eminent writers; and he always writes on basic matters.

In the 1850's he is drawn, often struggling, into the greatest social battle of his time, the battle over Negro slavery. Though he tries to turn away from it, he becomes more and more involved. The politics of compromise cannot hold him. He finds that the leading abolitionists have as bigoted a look as the Southern fire-eaters, and he longs to cry, "A plague on both your houses." However, the Fugitive Slave Law brings slavery home to Massachusetts and

Concord. The apolitical Emerson becomes a Republican and votes for Abraham Lincoln. He rejoices when Lincoln is elected President but regrets that he puts keeping the Union above the immediate abolition of slavery. However, when the Emancipation Proclamation comes from Lincoln's desk, Emerson is moved to celebrate a great day for his country and the world. When Lincoln is killed, he considers him a martyr.

The Civil War over, Emerson faces a new—and coarser— American age. Yet his reputation rises steadily. Honors accrue to him from all over the country. His lectures command fees higher than ever before. Though by the end of the war he is in his early sixties and has nothing new to say, audiences hurry to the hall when he reads his lectures and readers buy them in book form with almost equal alacrity. He has become an American institution. And an international one, for that matter. When he revisits the British Isles and the continent of Europe, further honors are heaped on him.

The grosser and more materialistic that nineteenth-century America becomes, the more it guiltily honors him. It realizes only gradually that it is honoring a shell. By his late sixties Emerson's memory is slipping; by his mid-seventies it is gone. Yet he still reads a lecture on occasion, shuffling through his papers. A devoted daughter acts as his secretary and guide, with much help from a young man named James Elliot Cabot. The two of them put together the final volumes of Emerson's writings, *Society and Solitude* (1870) and *Letters and Social Aims* (1876). Yet his end is not a grim one. He still has flashes of insight. He recognizes friends and family during his lucid intervals. He is nearly seventy-nine years old when he dies quietly on April 27, 1882. He has long since become an American Olympian.

With the passing of the decades Emerson's ideas have stayed alive. If they have not possessed the mounting persuasiveness of Henry Thoreau's, they still have kept an appeal of their own.

Emerson's essays too have remained in the anthologies and are read wherever American literature and thought are studied. And yet the impact of his person has grown fainter. The modern biographers who write eagerly about Melville or Mark Twain neglect Emerson. The last full-dress biography appeared in 1949. For America today his life seems to have lost much of its meaning.

During his own time, on the other hand, his character and actions meant a great deal; he was a national and indeed an international figure. Despite his misgivings about his lack of warmth, he aroused friendship and admiration in many who knew him. In the pages that follow we can see what kind of man he was. We have the reminiscences of old acquaintances represented here. We have the testimony of some who saw him lecture or heard him preach. We have several studies, from later writers, of illuminating episodes in his career. All this testimony is favorable, and understandably so; for Emerson, as we have said, was something of a saint. Nevertheless, he was far from bland. He aroused considerable opposition in his day, though none cogent enough to make it survive. And in our time he has encountered at least a few dissenters; we include in this volume selections from two of the most judicious ones.

My debt to my Emerson seminar at the University of Maryland is a recurring one and I am happy to record the fact. I am grateful for the secretarial help I received from Mrs. Paul Chadha, Miss Judith Clark, Miss Linda Koelker, and Miss Donna Waigand and the research assistance from Mr. George Bell, all of the University of Maryland. Also, I am indebted to the *Modern Language Review,* for I relied in my introduction on the reviews I have published there of the Emerson journals.

CARL BODE

University of Maryland
August 1968

RALPH WALDO EMERSON

Some Recollections of
Ralph Waldo Emerson

It is impossible for those who only knew Emerson through his writings to understand the peculiar love and veneration felt for him by those who knew him personally. Only by intercourse with him could the singular force, sweetness, elevation, originality, and comprehensiveness of his nature be fully appreciated; and the friend or acquaintance, however he might differ from him in opinion, felt the peculiar fascination of his character, and revolved around this solar mind in obedience to the law of spiritual gravitation—the spiritual law operating, like the natural law, directly as the mass, and inversely as the square of the distance. The friends nearest to him loved and honored him most; but those who only met him occasionally felt the attraction of his spiritual power, and could not mention him without a tribute of respect. There probably never was another man of the first class, with a general

---

In this general appreciation of Emerson we see reflections of the author's own background, for Whipple was a famous lecturer and critic in the mid-nineteenth century. He wrote on both American and English literature, displaying a bias in favor of the native product. His essay on Emerson is flawed by its adulation and exclamatory tone, but it helps us to see him as a person. The essay is reprinted from *Harper's Magazine*, LXV (September 1882), 576–587.

system of thought at variance with accredited opinions, who exercised so much gentle, persuasive power over the minds of his opponents. By declining all temptations to controversy he never raised the ferocious spirit which controversy engenders; he went on, year after year, in affirming certain spiritual facts which had been revealed to him when his soul was on the heights of spiritual contemplation; and if he differed from other minds, he thought it ridiculous to attempt to convert them to his individual insight and experience by *arguments* against their individual insights and their individual experiences. To his readers in the closet, and his hearers on the lecture platform, he poured lavishly out from his intellectual treasury—from the seemingly exhaustless Fortunatus' purse of his mind—the silver and gold, the pearls, rubies, amethysts, opals, and diamonds of thought. If his readers and his audiences chose to pick them up, they were welcome to them; but if they conceived he was deceiving them with sham jewelry, he would not condescend to explain the laborious processes in the mines of meditation by which he had brought the hidden treasures to light. I never shall forget his curt answer to a superficial auditor of one of his lectures. The critic was the intellectual busybody of the place, dipping into everything, knowing nothing, but contriving by his immense loquacity to lead the opinion of the town. "Now, Mr. Emerson," he said, "I appreciated much of your lecture, but I should like to speak to you of certain things in it which did not command my assent and approbation." Emerson turned to him, gave him one of his piercing looks, and replied, "Mr. ——, if anything I have spoken this evening met your mood, it is well; if it did not, I must tell you that I never argue on these high questions"; and as he thus somewhat haughtily escaped from his would-be querist, he cared little that this gossip and chatterer about philosophy and religion would exert all his influence to prevent Emerson from ever lecturing again in that town.

Indeed, everybody who intimately knew this seer and thinker

had the good sense never to intrude into the inward sanctities and privacies of his individual meditations, and vulgarly ask questions as to the doubts and conflicts he had encountered in that utter loneliness of thought, where his individual soul, in direct contact, as he supposed, with the "Over-Soul," was trying to solve problems of existence which perplex all thoughtful minds. He would do nothing more than make affirmations regarding the deep things of the spirit, which were to be accepted or rejected as they happened to strike or miss the point of inlet into the other intellects he addressed.

This austere reticence was consistent with the most perfect sincerity. Indeed, Emerson preached sincerity as among the first of virtues. He never hesitated to tell the poets, prose writers, reformers, "fanatics," who were his friends and acquaintances, exactly what he thought of them, and there was never a doubt of his mental and moral honesty in their reception of his criticism. He could afford to be sincere, for everybody felt that there was no taint of envy, jealousy, or malice in his nature. When he frankly told such men as Longfellow, Lowell, Holmes, and Whittier that in a particular poem they did not come up to his high ideal of what a poet should be and do, they assented to the criticism, and never dreamed that his judgment was influenced by the failure of his own poetry to attract that public attention which was righteously due to its vital excellence; for they all cordially agreed in thinking that he was the greatest poet the country had produced. There is not a solitary instance of his hesitating, kindly disapprobation of a writer who ranked among his associates which did not make the writer grateful to Emerson for his criticism, and which did not make him sensible that nothing base or mean could have prompted it. So it was with the ardent reformers. Garrison and Phillips, not to mention others, instinctively felt that Emerson was a man not to be assailed when he differed from them in their method of applying to affairs the moral sentiment of which Emerson was the most eloquent and authoritative spokesman; not, indeed, a voice crying in the wilderness, but a voice which seemed to utter eternal decrees, coming from the serene communion of the speaker with the very source of moral law.

The native elevation of Emerson's mind and the general loftiness of his thinking have sometimes blinded his admirers to the fact that he was one of the shrewdest of practical observers, and was capable of meeting so-called practical men on the level of the facts and principles which they relied upon for success in life. When I first had the happiness to make his acquaintance I was a clerk in a banking house. I have a faint memory of having written in a penny paper a notice of his first volume of *Essays* which differed altogether from the notices which appeared in business journals of a higher rank and price. The first thing that struck me was the quaint, keen, homely good sense which was one of the marked characteristics of the volume; and I contrasted the coolness of this transcendentalist, whenever he discussed matters relating to the conduct of life, with the fury of delusion under which merchants of established reputation sometimes seemed to be laboring in their mad attempts to resist the operation of the natural laws of trade. They, I thought, were the transcendentalists, the subjective poets, the Rousseaus and Byrons of business, who in their greed were fiercely "accommodating the shows of things to the desires of the mind," without any practical insight of principles or foresight of consequences. Nothing more amazed me, when I was a clerk, recording transactions in which I incurred no personal responsibility, than the fanaticism of capitalists in venturing their money in wild speculations. The willingness to buy waste and worthless Eastern lands; the madness of the men who sunk their millions in certain railroads; and the manias which occasionally seize upon and passionately possess businessmen, surpassing in folly those fine frenzies of the imagination which are considered to lead to absurdities belonging to poets alone; all these facts early impressed me with the conviction that a transcendentalist of the type of Emerson was as good a judge of investments on earth as he was of investments in the heavens above the earth.

As far as my memory serves me at this time, I think to me, in my youthful presumption, belongs the dubious honor or dishonor of calling him our "Greek-Yankee—a cross between Plato and Jonathan Slick." I am less certain as to the other statement that he was "a Hindoo-Yankee—a cross between Brahma and Poor Richard"; and there are so many competitors for the distinction of originating these epigrammatic impertinences that I should no more dare to present my claims to priority in inventing them than to reopen the controversy respecting the authorship of "Beautiful Snow" or "Rock Me to Sleep, Mother." But I always wondered that the Franklin side of his opulent and genial nature did not draw to him a host of readers who might be repelled by the dazzling though puzzling sentences in which his ideal philosophy found expression. It is to be supposed that such persons refused to read him because they distrusted his constant tendency to combine beauty with use. The sense of beauty, indeed, was so vital an element in the very constitution of his being that it decorated everything it touched. He was a thorough artist, while inculcating maxims of thrift far beyond those of Poor Richard. His beautiful genius could not be suppressed even when he discoursed of the ugliest sides of a farmer's life; he shed an ideal light over pots and cans, over manure heaps and cattle raising; and when he announced that maxim of celestial prudence, "Hitch your wagon to a star," the transcendentalist was discovered peeping through the economist, and it became hard to believe that he was in ordinary affairs a really practical man. He should have stuck, the economists said, to the wagon, and left out the star, though the

introduction of the star was really the most practical thing in his
quaint statement of the vital dependence of individual thrift on
directing and all-embracing law.

The raciest testimony that ever came within my knowledge as to
the soundness of Emerson in practical matters was delivered by a
sturdy, stalwart Vermonter in a car on the Fitchburg Railroad. My
journey was to be a tedious one of three hundred miles, and when
I took my seat in the car, I felt that my fellow-passengers would
give me no such glimpses into their characters as would be afforded
by a ride of ten miles in a stagecoach. In a railroad car the passengers are gloomily reticent, as if they expected to be launched into
eternity at any moment; in a stage they indulge in all the fury of
gossip, and reveal themselves while praising or censuring others.
There were two persons in front of me, mighty in bulk, but apparently too much absorbed in their own reflections to speak to
each other. The train, as usual, stopped at Concord. Then one of
the giants turned to the other, and lazily remarked, "Mr. Emerson,
I hear, lives in this town."

"Ya-as," was the drawling rejoinder; "and I understand that, in
spite of his odd notions, he is a man of *con-sid-er*-able propity."

This apposite judgment was made when Emerson's essays had
been translated into most of the languages of Europe, and when
the recognition of his genius was even more cordial abroad than
it was among his few thousands of appreciative admirers at home;
but the shrewd Yankee who uttered it was more impressed by his
thrift than by his thinking. He belonged to the respectable race of
*de*scendentalists, and was evidently puzzled to understand how a
*tran*scendentalist could acquire "propity."

On one occasion, in my early acquaintance with Emerson, I was
hastily summoned to lecture at a country town some five miles
from Boston, because Emerson, who had been expected to occupy
the desk, had not signified his acceptance of the invitation. He
either had neglected to answer the letter of the committee, or his

own note in reply had miscarried. About ten minutes before the lecture was to begin, Emerson appeared. Of course I insisted on having the privilege of listening to him, rather than compel the audience to listen to me. He generously declared that as the mistake seemed to have arisen from his own neglect, I had the right to the platform. When I solemnly assured him that no lecture would be heard that evening in that town unless he delivered it, he, still somewhat protesting, unrolled his manuscript, and took his place at the desk. The lecture, though perhaps not one of his best Lyceum discourses, was better than the best of any other living lecturer. When it was over, he invited me to take a seat in the chaise which had brought him from Boston. I gladly accepted. The horse was, fortunately for me, one of the slowest beasts whichever had the assurance to pretend to convey faster, by carriage, two persons from one point to another than an ordinary pedestrian could accomplish in a meditative walk. The pace was, I think, about two miles an hour. As soon as we got into the chaise, I began to speak of the lecture, and referring to what he had said of the Puritans, I incidentally alluded to the peculiar felicity of his use of the word "grim," and added that I noticed it was a favorite word of his in his published essays. "Do you say," he eagerly responded, "that I use the word often?" "Yes," I replied, "but never without its being applicable to the class of persons you are characterizing." He reflected a minute or two, and then said, as if he had experienced a pang of intellectual remorse, "The word is probably passing with me into a mannerism, and I must hereafter guard against it—must banish it from my dictionary."

By this time we had passed out of the town into the long country road which led to Boston. Emerson was in his happiest mood. He entered into a peculiar kind of conversation with his young companion, in which reverie occasionally emerged into soliloquy, and then again became a real talk between the two, though ever liable to subside into reverie and soliloquy if his interlocutor had tact enough to restrain his own tendency to self-expression. I shall never forget that evening. The moon was nearly at its full, undisturbed by a cloud, and the magical moonlight flooded the landscape and skyscape with its soft, gentle, serene, mystical radiance, making strangely unreal all things which seem so substantial when viewed in the "insolent," revealing glare of the sun. Astronomers tell us that the moon is a dead body, all its central fires burned out, and swinging in space as a lifeless mass of matter, good for nothing except to give us light for about half the nights of every month in the year, or to illustrate the operation of the law of gravitation; but of all the lights in the solar or stellar system it is pre-eminently the idealist and transcendentalist of the tenants of the sky; and I never felt its mystical charm more profoundly than on this ride of two hours with Emerson. The lazy horse seemed to be indulging in the luxury of his own reflections, and was only kept from stopping altogether and setting up as a philosopher on his own account, renouncing his ignominious bondage to harness and bridle, by the occasional idle flap of Emerson's whip on his hide—a stimulant to exertion which was so light that I thought its full force could not have broken the backbone of an ordinary fly. So we "tooled on." The conversation at last drifted to contemporary actors who assumed to personate leading characters in Shakespeare's greatest plays. Had I ever seen an actor who satisfied me when he pretended to be Hamlet or Othello, Lear or Macbeth? Yes, I had seen the elder Booth in these characters. Though not perfect, he approached nearer to perfection than any other actor I knew. Nobody, of course, could really satisfy a student of Shakespeare. Still I thought that the elder Booth had a realizing imagination, that he conceived the nature of the person he embodied in its essential individual qualities, that so firm and true was his imaginative grasp of a character that he preserved the unity of one of Shakespeare's complex natures while giving all the varieties of its manifestation. Macready might be the more popular actor of the two, at least in all "refined" circles; but the trouble with Macready was that, while he was gifted with a good understanding, he was strangely deficient in impassioned imagination, and that he accordingly, by a logical process, inferred the character he wished to impersonate by a patient study of Shakespeare's text, and then played the inference.

"Ah," said Emerson, giving a tender touch of his whip to the indolent horse—an animal who, during the three minutes I consumed in eulogizing Booth, showed a natural disposition to go to sleep—"I see you are one of the happy mortals who are capable of being carried away by an actor of Shakespeare. Now whenever I visit the theater to witness the performance of one of his dramas, I am carried away by the poet. I went last Tuesday to see Macready in *Hamlet*. I got along very well until he came to the passage:

> thou, dead corse, again, in complete steel,
> Revisit'st thus the glimpses of the moon

and then actor, theater, all vanished in view of that solving and dissolving imagination, which could reduce this big globe and all it inherits into mere 'glimpses of the moon.' The play went on, but, absorbed in this one thought of the mighty master, I paid no heed to it."

What specially impressed me, as Emerson was speaking, was his glance at our surroundings as he slowly uttered "glimpses of the moon"; for here above us was the same moon which must have given birth to Shakespeare's thought, its soft rays of consecrating light insinuating a skeptical doubt of the real existence of the world of matter, which, in the fierce glow of the noontide sun, appears so imperturbably conscious of a solid, incontestable reality.

Afterward, in his lecture on Shakespeare, Emerson made use of the thought suggested in our ride by moonlight. He said: "That imagination which dilates the closet he writes in to the world's dimensions, crowds it with agents in rank and order, as quickly

reduces the big reality to be the 'glimpses of the moon.' " It seems
to me that his expression of the thought, as it occurred to him
when he felt the enchantment of the moonlight palpably present to
his eyes and imagination, is better in my version than in the comparatively cold language in which he afterward embodied it. But in
the printed lecture there is one sentence declaring the absolute insufficiency of any actor, in any theater, to fix attention on himself
while uttering Shakespeare's words, which seems to me the most
exquisite statement ever made of the magical suggestiveness of
Shakespeare's expression. I have often quoted it, but it will bear
quotation again and again, as the best prose sentence ever written
on this side of the Atlantic. "The recitation begins; one golden
word leaps out immortal from all this painted pedantry, *and sweet-
ly torments us with invitations to its own inaccessible homes.*"

Emerson's voice had a strange power, which affected me more
than any other voice I ever heard on the stage or on the platform.
It was pure thought translated into purely intellectual tone, the
perfect music of spiritual utterance. It is impossible to read his
verses adequately without bearing in mind his peculiar accent and
emphasis; and some of the grandest and most uplifting passages in
his prose lose much of their effect unless the reader can recall the
tones of his voice—a voice now, alas! silent on earth forever, but
worthy of being heard in that celestial company which he, "a spirit
of the largest size and divinest mettle," has now exchanged for his
earthly companions. There was nothing sensual, nothing even sensuous, nothing weakly melodious, in his utterance; but his voice
had the stern, keen, penetrating sweetness which made it a fit organ
for his self-centered, commanding mind. Yet though peculiar to
himself, it had at the same time an impersonal character, as though
a spirit was speaking through him. Thus in his lecture on Swedenborg he began with a compact statement of the opinions of the
Swedish sage—opinions which seemed to be wide enough to compel all men, pagans and Christians, to assent to his dogmatic state-

ments. The exposition was becoming monotonous after the lapse of a quarter of an hour. The audience supposed that he was a convert to the Swedenborgian doctrines. At the conclusion of his exposition he paused for half a minute, and then, in his highest, most piercing tones, he put the question, "*Who is* EMANUEL SWEDENBORG?" his voice rising as he accented every syllable. The effect was electric. Many persons in the audience who had begun to betray a decided disposition to go to sleep waked up. The lecturer then proceeded to give, in short, flashing sentences, a criticism of the Swedenborgian ideas, which seemed to have bored him as they undoubtedly bored many of his hearers, and everybody present eagerly listened to the objections which rendered it reasonable for them to recognize Swedenborg as a very great representative man, without making it necessary for them to abandon the churches to which they were attached and swell the congregations of those of the New Jerusalem.

Again, after reciting the marvels of Shakespeare's genius, placing him above all other writers, he came to the consideration of the serious side of this greatest of poets. What did he teach? "He converted the elements, which waited on his command, into entertainments. He was master of the revels to mankind. Is it not as if one should have, through majestic powers of science, the comets given into his hand, or the planets and their moons, and should draw them from their orbits to glare with the municipal fireworks on a holiday night, and advertise in all towns, 'very superior pyrotechny this evening'?" All this was delivered in an intense and penetrating yet somewhat subdued tone, and it is hardly possible to convey by printers' ink and types the gradual rise of his voice as he added: "One remembers again the trumpet text in the Koran, 'The heavens and the earth, and all that is between them, *think ye we have* CREATED THEM IN JEST?" It is only by a typographical rise from italics to capitals that the faintest indication can be conveyed of the upward march of his voice as it finally pealed forth in "jest."

In another lecture he had occasion to refer to what Mr. Choate had called "the glittering generalities of the Declaration of Independence." If a printer could put it into the smallest type possible to be read by the aid of the microscope, he could not fitly show the scorn embodied in the first part of the sentence in which Emerson replied; nor could the same printer's largest types suggest an idea of the triumphant tone, shot as from a vocal ten-inch gun, in which he gave the second portion of it: "Glittering generalities!— *rather* BLAZING UBIQUITIES!"

Emerson's generous and thorough appreciation of the genius and character of Henry D. Thoreau was shown in many ways and on many occasions. At my first or second visit to Concord, as a lecturer before its Lyceum, he said to me, in the quaint condensed fashion of speech in which he always sketched an original character: "You should know Thoreau. He became disgusted with our monotonous civilization, and went, self-banished, to our Walden woods. There he lives. He built his own hut, cooks his own food, refuses to pay taxes, reads Aeschylus, abjures models, and is a great man." From my first introduction, Thoreau seemed to me a man who had experienced Nature as other men are said to have experienced religion. An unmistakable courage, sincerity, and manliness breathed in every word he uttered. I once met him and Mr. Alcott in State Street, in the busiest hour of the day, while I was hurrying to a bank. They had paused before a saloon to get a glimpse of the crowds of merchants and brokers passing up and down the street. "Ah!" I laughingly said, after shaking hands, "I see it is eleven o'clock, and you are going to take a drink." Mr. Alcott, in his sweetest and most serene tones, replied for both: "No; vulgar and ordinary stimulants are not for us. But if you can show us a place where we can drink Bacchus himself, the soul of the inspiration of the poet and the seer, we shall be your debtors forever." There is hardly any biography recently published more interesting than Mr. Sanborn's life of Thoreau; for Mr. Sanborn knew him so intimately that he gives us an "interior" view of the remarkable person he has taken for his subject. Indeed, what can be more interesting than the spectacle of a man whose independence was so rooted in his nature that he coolly set up his private opinion against the average opinion of the human race, and contrived so to incorporate his opinion into his daily life that he came out in the end a victor in the contest? And in respect to the sympathy that Nature had for *him*, in return for his sympathy with *her*, one feels that he must have been in Emerson's mind when he celebrated, in "Wood Notes," his "forest seer":

> It seemed as if the breezes brought him;
> It seemed as if the sparrows taught him;
> As if by secret sight he knew
>   Where, in far fields, the orchis grew.
> Many haps fall in the field,
>   Seldom seen by wishful eyes;
> But all her shows did Nature yield
>   To please and win this pilgrim wise.
> He saw the partridge drum in the woods;
>   He heard the woodcock's evening hymn;
> He found the tawny thrush's broods;
>   *And the shy hawk did wait for him;*
> What others did at distance hear,
>   And guessed within the thicket's gloom,
> Was showed to this philosopher,
>   And at his bidding seemed to come.

Miss Fredrika Bremer, in her book recording her tour in the United States, took unwarrantable liberties in describing the households of those persons whose hospitalities she enjoyed. Emerson was specially annoyed at her chatter about him and his family. What vexed him most, however, was her reference to Samuel Hoar, a man whom Emerson, as well as all other citizens of Concord, held in distinguished honor as the living embodiment of integrity, intelligence, wisdom, piety, and benevolence. Emerson's well-known quatrain, with the simple title "S. H.," is a monument to this good and wise man's memory:

> With beams December's planets dart
>   His cold eye truth and conduct scanned;
> July was in his sunny heart,
>   October in his liberal hand.

Yet this venerable sage, whose native dignity should have shielded him from the impertinence of even a gossip so incorrigible as Miss Bremer, was represented in that lady's book as a garrulous old gentleman who, at his own table, to which she was an invited guest, had made in lieu of the ordinary grace a prayer which she considered so long as to be tiresome. "As if," said Emerson to me, in his deepest indignant tone—"as if Mr. Hoar was expected to pray for her entertainment!"

He had, from the start, a strong antipathy to "spiritism." When departed spirits, by "knockings" and moving furniture, first began to inform us poor mortals that they were still alive—alive, however, in a world which appeared, on the whole, to be worse than that from which death had released them, the great question of immortality was considered by many pious persons to have obtained new evidences of its truth from these materialistic manifestations. Emerson's feeling was that so exquisitely expressed by Tennyson:

> How pure at heart and sound in head,
>   With what divine affections bold,
>   Should be the man whose thought would hold
> An hour's communion with the dead!
>
> In vain shalt thou, or any, call
>   The spirits from their golden day,
>   Except, like them, thou too canst say,
> My spirit is at peace with all.

> They haunt the silence of the breast,
> Imaginations calm and fair,
> The memory like a cloudless air,
> The conscience as a sea at rest.

Emerson's impatience when the subject came up for discussion in a company of intelligent people was amusing to witness. He was specially indignant at the idea of women adopting spiritism as a profession, and engaging to furnish all people with news of their deceased friends at a shilling a head. The enormous vulgarity of the whole thing impressed him painfully, especially when he was told that some of his own friends paid even the slightest attention to the revelations, as he phrased it, of "those seamstresses turned into sibyls, who charged a pistareen a spasm!" Brougham's well-known remark that the idea of Campbell's writing his life added a new horror to death, was a just anticipation of a terrible fact; for Campbell did write his life, and made a dreadful wreck of Brougham's reputation. Happily, Emerson's last days were clouded by a failure of memory, or he might have mourned that his spirit would be called by "mediums" from "its golden day" to furnish the public with information detailing his present "gossip about the celestial politics," translated from the terse and beautiful language in which he was accustomed to speak his thoughts on earth into the peculiar dialect which uneducated mediums generally use in their rapt communion with the spirits of such men as Bacon, Milton, Webster, and Channing—spirits who, as far as their style of expression and elevation of thought are concerned, appear to have found their immortality a curse—spirits who have dwindled in mental stature just in proportion as they have ascended into the region of incorporeal existence—spirits not made perfect but decidedly *im*perfect in heaven.

After his return from his second visit to England, in 1847, I had a natural wish to learn his impressions of the distinguished men he had met. His judgment of Tennyson was this, that he was the most "satisfying" of the men of letters he had seen. He witnessed one of Macaulay's brilliant feats in conversation at a dinner where Hallam was one of the guests. The talk was on the question whether the "additional letters" of Oliver Cromwell, lately published by Carlyle, were spurious or genuine. "For my part," said Emerson, "the suspicious fact about them was this, that they all seemed written to sustain Mr. Carlyle's view of Cromwell's character; but the discussion turned on the external evidences of their being forgeries. Macaulay overcame everybody at the table, including Hallam, by pouring out with \   rious volubility instances of the use of words in a different meaning from that they bore in Cromwell's time, or by citing words which were not in use at all until half a century later. A question which might have been settled in a few minutes by the consent of a few men of insight opened a tiresome controversy which lasted during the whole dinner. Macaulay seemed to have the best of it; still, I did not like the arrogance with which he paraded his minute information; but then there was a fire, speed, fury, talent, and effrontery in the fellow which were very taking." When Emerson, on his return, made in his *English Traits* his short, contemptuous criticism on Macaulay as a writer representing the material rather than the spiritual interests of England, it is evident that the verbal bullet hit the object at which it was aimed in the white. "The brilliant Macaulay, who expresses the tone of the English governing classes of the day, explicitly teaches that *good* means good to eat, good to wear, material commodity; that the glory of modern philosophy is its direction or 'fruit'; to yield economical inventions; and that its merit is to avoid ideas and to avoid morals. He thinks it the distinctive merit of the Baconian philosophy, in its triumph over the old Platonic, its disentangling the intellect from theories of the all-Fair and the all-Good, and pinning it down to the making a better sick-chair and a better wine-whey for an invalid; this not ironically, but in good faith; that 'solid advantage,' as he calls it—meaning always sensual benefit—is the only good." This criticism, though keen, is undoubtedly one-sided. Macaulay felt it. In the height of his fame, in January, 1850, he writes in his diary: "Many readers give credit for profundity to whatever is obscure, and call all that is perspicuous shallow. But *coragio!* and think of A.D. 2850. Where will your Emersons be then?" Well, it may be confidently predicted, they will at least march abreast of the Macaulays.

In all Emerson's experience as a lecturer there was only one occasion when he received that tribute to a radical orator's timely eloquence which is expressed in hisses. The passage of the Fugitive Slave Law stirred him into unwonted moral passion and righteous wrath. He accepted an invitation to deliver a lecture in Cambridgeport, called for the purpose of protesting against that infamous anomaly in jurisprudence and insult to justice which had the impudence to call itself a law. Those who sympathized with him were there in force; but a score or two of foolish Harvard students came down from the college to the hall where the lecture was delivered, determined to assert "the rights of the South," and to preserve the threatened Union of the States. They were the rowdiest, noisiest, most brainless set of young gentlemen that ever pretended to be engaged in studying "the humanities" at the chief university of the country. Their only arguments were hisses and groans whenever the most illustrious of American men of letters uttered an opinion which expressed the general opinion of the civilized world. If he quoted Coke, Holt, Blackstone, Mansfield, they hissed all these sages of the law because their judgments came from the illegal lips of Emerson. It was curious to watch him as, at each point he made, he paused to let the storm of hisses subside. The noise was something he had never heard before; there was a queer, quizzical, squirrel-like or birdlike expression in his eye as he calmly looked round to see what strange human animals were present to make such sounds; and when he proceeded to utter another indisputable truth, and it was responded to by another chorus

of hisses, he seemed absolutely to enjoy the new sensation he experienced, and waited for these signs of disapprobation to stop
altogether before he resumed his discourse. The experience was
novel; still there was not the slightest tremor in his voice, not even
a trace of the passionate resentment which a speaker under such
circumstances and impediments usually feels, and which urges him
into the cheap retort about serpents, but a quiet waiting for the
time when he should be allowed to go on with the next sentence.
During the whole evening he never uttered a word which was not
written down in the manuscript from which he read. Many of us
at the time urged Emerson to publish the lecture; ten or fifteen
years after, when he was selecting material for a new volume of
essays, I entreated him to include in it the old lecture at Cambridgeport; but he, after deliberation, refused, feeling probably
that being written under the impulse of the passion of the day, it
was no fit and fair summary of the characters of the statesmen he
assailed. Of one passage in the lecture I preserve a vivid remembrance. After affirming that the eternal law of righteousness, which
rules all created things, nullified the enactment of Congress, and
after citing the opinions of several magnates of jurisprudence, that
immoral laws are void and of no effect, he slowly added, in a
scorching and biting irony of tone which no words can describe,
"but still a little Episcopalian clergyman assured me yesterday that
the Fugitive Slave Law must be obeyed and enforced." After the
lapse of thirty years, the immense humor of bringing all the forces
of nature, all the principles of religion, and all the decisions of
jurists to bear with their Atlas weight on the shoulders of one poor
little conceited clergyman to crush him to atoms, and he in his in-
nocence not conscious of it, makes me laugh now as all the audience laughed then, the belligerent Harvard students included.

Emerson's good sense was so strong that it always seemed to be
specially awakened in the company of those who were most in
sympathy with his loftiest thinking. Thus, when "the radical philos-

ophers" were gathered one evening at his house, the conversation naturally turned on the various schemes of benevolent people to reform the world. Each person present had a panacea to cure all the distempers of society. For hours the talk ran on, and before bedtime came, all the sin and misery of the world had been apparently expelled from it, and our planet was reformed and transformed into an abode of human angels, and virtue and happiness were the lot of each human being. Emerson listened, but was sparing of speech. Probably he felt, with Lamennais, that if facts did not resist thoughts, the earth would in a short time become uninhabitable. At any rate, he closed the *séance* with the remark: "A few of us old codgers meet at the fireside on a pleasant evening, and in thought and hope career, balloonlike, over the whole universe of matter and mind, finding no resistance to our theories, because we have, in the sweet delirium of our thinking, none of those obstructive facts which face the practical reformer the moment he takes a single forward step; then we go to bed; and the pity of it is we wake up in the morning feeling that we are the same poor old imbeciles we were before!"

A transcendentalist is sometimes compelled, by what Cowley calls "the low conveniencies of fate," to subordinate the principles of his system of thought to the practical exigency of the hour. A curious illustration of this fact occurred, some fifteen or twenty years ago, in the early days of the "Saturday Club." After some preliminary skirmishing, Emerson asked Agassiz to give him a short exposition of his leading ideas as a naturalist in respect to what was known of the genesis of things. Agassiz, in his vehement, rapid way, began at the microscopic "cell," beyond which no discovered instrument of investigation could go, and proceeded to show the gradual ascent from this "cell" to the highest forms of animal life. He took about half an hour in making his condensed statement, and then Emerson's turn began. "But, Mr. Agassiz, I see that all your philosophy is under the law of succession; it is genealogical; it is based on the reality of time; but you must know that some of us believe with Kant that time is merely a subjective form of human thought, having no objective existence." Then suddenly taking out his watch, and learning that he had only fifteen minutes to get to the Fitchburg Railroad in order to be in "time" to catch the last train to Concord on that afternoon, he took his hat, swiftly donned his overcoat, and as he almost rushed from the room he assured Agassiz that he would discuss the subject at some other "time," when he was less pressed by his engagements at home. For years afterward, when the transcendentalist met the naturalist at the club, I watched in vain for a recurrence of the controversy. I do not think it was ever reopened between them.

Many of Emerson's friends and acquaintances thought that his sense of humor was almost as keen as his sense of Beauty and his sense of Right. I do not remember an instance in my conversations with him, when the question came up of his being not understood, or, what is worse, misunderstood by the public, that he did not treat the matter in an exquisitely humorous way, telling the story of his defeats in making himself comprehended by the audience or the readers he addressed as if the misapprehensions of his meaning were properly subjects of mirth, in which he could heartily join. This is the test of the humorist, that he can laugh *with* those who laugh *at* him. For example, on one occasion I recollect saying that of all his college addresses I thought the best was that on "The Method of Nature," delivered before the Society of the Adelphi, in Waterville College, Maine, August 11, 1841. He then gave me a most amusing account of the circumstances under which the oration was delivered. It seems that after conceiving the general idea of the address, he banished himself to Nantasket Beach, secluded himself for a fortnight in a room in the public house, the windows of which looked out on the ocean, moving from his chamber and writing desk only to take early morning and late evening walks on the beach; and thought, at the end, he had produced something which was worthy of being listened to even by the Society of the Adelphi. At that time a considerable portion of the journey to Waterville had to be made by stage. He arrived late in the evening, travel-worn and tired out, when almost all the sober inhabitants of Waterville had gone to bed. It appeared that there was some doubt as to the particular citizen's house at which he was to pass the night. "The stage-driver," said Emerson, "stopped at one door; rapped loudly; a window was opened; something in a nightgown asked what he wanted; the stage-driver replied that he had inside a man who *said* he was to deliver the lit-ra-rye oration tomorrow, and thought he was to stop there; but the nightgown disappeared, with the chilling remark that he was not to stay at *his* house. Then we went to another, and still another, dwelling, rapped, saw similar nightgowns and heard similar voices at similar raised windows; and it was only after repeated disturbances of the peace of the place that the right house was hit, where I found a hospitable reception. The next day I delivered my oration, which was heard with cold, silent, unresponsive attention, in which there seemed to be a continuous unuttered rebuke and protest. The services were closed by prayer, and the good man who prayed, prayed for the orator, but also warned his hearers against heresies and wild notions, which appeared to me of that kind for which I was held responsible. The address was really written in the heat and happiness of what I thought a real inspiration; but all the warmth was extinguished in that lake of iced water." The conversation occurred so long ago that I do not pretend to give Emerson's exact words, but this was the substance of his ludicrous statement of the rapture with which he had written what was so frigidly received. He seemed intensely to enjoy the fun of his material discomforts and his spiritual discomfiture.

Emerson had some strange tastes and some equally strange distastes in regard to poets. Usually his criticism was wonderfully acute and accurate, compressing into a few significant words what other critics would fail to convey in an elaborate analysis. He darted by a combination of insight and instinct to the exact point in a poet's writings where the poetry in him was best embodied and expressed; and his reading of the passages which had most impressed him excelled that of the most accomplished professional elocutionist I ever listened to. But he never could endure Shelley, and declared that if the objections of practical men to poetry rested on such poets as Shelley, he should cordially agree with them. He admitted, of course, the beauty of "The Skylark" and "The Cloud"; but as an apostle of hope and health and cheer, he could not pardon the note of lamentation which runs through Shelley's poetry, and thought that his gifts of imagination and melody, remarkable as they were, were no atonement for his unmanly wailing and sobbing over the ills of existence. A poet, he said, should invigorate, not depress, the soul. It was in vain to tell him that such ethereal powers of imagination and sentiment as Shelley possessed should be considered apart from the direction they happened to take, owing to the unfortunate circumstances of his life. No; he would discard such sick souls from his sympathy, as he would discard all sick bodies. He showed always a comical disgust of sick people generally. Everybody who heard his lecture called "Considerations by the Way," must remember the peculiar force and bitterness with which he described sickness "as a cannibal, which eats up all the life and youth it can lay hold of and absorbs its own sons and daughters. I figure it as a pale, wailing, distracted phantom, absolutely selfish, heedless of what is good and great, attentive to its own sensations, losing its soul, and afflicting other souls with meanness and mopings, and with ministrations to its voracity of trifles. Dr. Johnson severely said, 'Every man is a rascal as soon as he is sick.' " And then he went on to say that we should give the sick every aid, but not give them "ourselves." Then followed a cruelly wise remark, which shocked many in the audience, and the real import of which was taken only by a few. "I once asked a clergyman in a country town who were his companions? what men of ability he saw? He replied that he spent his time with the sick and the dying. I said he seemed to me to need quite other company, and all the more that he had this; for if people were sick and dying to any purpose, we would leave all and go to them, but, as far as I had observed, they were as frivolous as the rest, and sometimes much more frivolous." Every one who has observed how many conscientious clergymen are converted into nerveless moral valetudinarians, losing all power of communicating healthy moral life, by constantly acting as spiritual nurses to the sick, complaining, and ever-dying but never dead members of their parishes, must acknowledge the half-truth in this apparently harsh statement.

The feeling that it is the duty of the teacher of his fellow-men, whether preacher, poet, romancer, or philosopher, to console by cheering and invigorating them, entered into all his criticism. When *The Scarlet Letter,* in many respects the greatest romance of the century, was published, he conceded that it was a work of power; "but," he said to me, with a repulsive shrug of the shoulders as he uttered the word, "it is ghastly." It seemed to me that "ghostly" would be a more truthful characterization of it; but it was impossible to remove from his mind the general impression any book had left on it by arguments. "Ghastly!" he repeated—"ghastly!" He seemed quietly impregnable to any considerations respecting the masterly imaginative analysis which Hawthorne had displayed in depicting the spiritual moods of his guilty hero and heroine, and his keen perception of the outlying spiritual laws which, being violated in their sin, reacted with such terrible force in their punishment. The book left an unpleasant impression on him; that was enough, as it was enough to lead him to condemn Goethe's *Faust.*

In judging of works of immensely less importance, which only excited his ridicule, his irony was often delicious. Then there were popular books whose daily sale exceeded that of all his own volumes in ten years; these he spoke of with admirable humor and good humor. Talking with him once on the character of the first Napoleon, I asked him if he had read the Reverend Mr. Abbott's history of the exploits and objects of the Emperor. "Yes," he dryly answered; "and it has given to me an altogether original idea of that notable man. It seems to teach that the great object of Napoleon in all his wars was to establish in benighted Europe our New England system of Sunday schools. A book like that is invaluable; it revolutionizes all our notions of historical men."

In such recollections of Emerson as I have here recorded there has been, of course, no attempt to portray his character as a whole, but simply to exhibit some aspects of it. There was a side of his nature, or rather the very center of his nature—his "heart of heart"—on which I suppose even his intimate friends—with whom I do not presume to rank myself—would speak with a certain reserve. Dr. Bartol, one of these friends, whose beautiful tribute to Emerson has been published, hints of the loneliness of thought in which a large portion of his life was probably passed. The incommunicable elements in Emerson's spiritual experience must, indeed, have exceeded what he felt himself capable of communicating, not to speak of that portion he was indisposed to communicate. In one of his most characteristic essays there is a pregnant sentence in which he declares that, in its highest moods, "the soul gives itself, alone, original, and pure, to the Lonely, Original, and Pure, who, on that condition, gladly inhabits, leads, and speaks through it." This mystic communion of the soul with its source had, with him, a solemnity so sacred that it must needs be secret; it either exalted his mortal nature into a "beatitude past utterance," or depressed it with ominous misgivings and "obstinate questionings" which could find no adequate outlet in words; and though we detect in the noblest passages of his writings traces of this immediate personal communion with the Highest and the Divine, it is doubtful if he ever spoke of it to his nearest relations and friends. In this he differed from most men of profound religious genius, who are sometimes garrulous on those points where he was inexorably mute. He never exclaimed, as other pious souls have exclaimed, "See what the Lord has done for *me!*" His reticence was the modesty of spiritual manliness. What he felt on such high matters he felt to be ineffable and unutterable; but how awful must have been at times his sense of spiritual loneliness, his lips austerely shut even when the closest, dearest, and most trusted companions of his soul delicately hinted their wish he would speak; but he died and made no sign.

Still, at just one remove from the sacred secrecy of his inmost individual consciousness and experience, he is ever found to be the frankest of writers. Matthew Arnold has revived a phrase originally used by Swift in his "Battle of the Books," and made it stand as a mark of the perfection of intellectual character. It is curious that this phrase, "sweetness and light," should have been uttered by the greatest cynical apostle of bitterness and gloom who has left a record of his genius in English literature, and also uttered, as far as the side he took is concerned, in an ig-nominious literary brawl, in which he was the champion of Temple, Boyle, and Atterbury, against Bentley, the greatest scholar in Europe. Bentley was, of course, victor in the contest, even in the opinion of all candid scholars at first opposed to him.

But "sweetness and light" are precious and inspiring only so far as they express the essential sweetness of the disposition of the thinker, and the essential illuminating power of his intelligence. Emerson's greatness came from his character. Sweetness and light streamed from him because they were *in* him. In everything he thought, wrote, and did we feel the presence of a personality as vigorous and brave as it was sweet, and the particular radical thought he at any time expressed derived its power to animate and illuminate other minds from the might of the manhood which was

felt to be within and behind it. To "sweetness and light" he therefore added the prime quality of fearless manliness.

If the force of Emerson's character was thus inextricably
blended with the force of all his faculties of intellect and imagination, and the refinement of all his sentiments, we have still to
account for the peculiarities of his genius, and to answer the question, why do we instinctively apply the epithet "Emersonian" to
every characteristic passage in his writings? We are told that he
was the last in a long line of clergymen, his ancestors, and that
the modern doctrine of heredity accounts for the impressive emphasis he laid on the moral sentiment; but that does not solve
the puzzle why he unmistakably differed in his nature and genius
from all other Emersons. An imaginary genealogical chart of
descent connecting him with Confucius or Gotama would be more
satisfactory. At the time he acquired notoriety but had not yet
achieved fame, it was confidently asserted in all Boston circles
that his brother Charles, the "calm, chaste scholar" celebrated by
Holmes, was greatly his superior in ability, and would, had he not
died early, have entirely eclipsed Ralph; Emerson himself, the
most generous and loving of brothers, always inclined to this
opinion; but there is not an atom of evidence that Charles, had
he lived, would have produced works which would be read by a
choice company of thinkers and scholars all over the world,
which would be translated into all the languages of Europe, and
would be prized in London and Edinburgh, in Berlin and Vienna,
in Rome and Paris, as warmly as they were in Boston and New
York. What distinguishes *the* Emerson was his *exceptional* genius
and character, that something in him which separated him from all
other Emersons, as it separated him from all other eminent men
of letters, and impressed every intelligent reader with the feeling
that he was not only "original but aboriginal." Some traits of his
mind and character may be traced back to his ancestors, but what
doctrine of heredity can give us the genesis of his genius? Indeed,

the safest course to pursue is to quote his own words, and despairingly confess that it is the nature of genius "to spring, like the rainbow daughter of Wonder, from the invisible, to abolish the past, and refuse all history."

RALPH L. RUSK

★

Emerson in Love

Ellen Louisa Tucker was only seventeen years old but had surprising dignity in spite of her youthfulness and her delicate, very feminine figure. A fine forehead and eyes gave her firmly molded oval face the appearance of intelligence as well as eagerness. She had the air of a girl that knew her own mind, and she probably knew better than Waldo Emerson what was going on in his when he arrived in the town of Concord, New Hampshire. He reasoned it out that he had arranged to preach to the local Unitarian congregation for a few Sundays in order to give his brother Edward a chance to rest in the country; but Ellen doubtless knew she was the magnet that brought him there. This was not his only visit to the northern Concord since he had met her on the last Christmas Day. What came of the sleighing party to the neighboring Shaker village of Canterbury soon after their first meeting is not clear, but they were probably together then. In the spring, when green foliage softened the severe New Hampshire landscape,

Undoubtedly the most human episode in Emerson's life was his courtship of and marriage to Ellen Tucker. Here it is pictured in the best and most scholarly biography that we have so far, Rusk's *The Life of Ralph Waldo Emerson* (1949). The story is abridged from the chapter "Ellen" and is reprinted with the permission of the Columbia University Press. Rusk himself was long a professor of American literature at Columbia, where he specialized in New England transcendentalism.

28

he made new visits to her town, and by then any well-informed gossip in the neighborhood would probably have concluded that they were in love. . . .

Now, in December, when, at least in Ellen's view of the matter, their love affair was of long standing, Waldo Emerson may actually have believed that he had got over his "blushes & wishes," as he said, before returning to "that dangerous neighborhood." But if so he was quickly disillusioned. The twenty-five-year-old philosopher made only an inglorious attempt to be philosophical about Ellen. He was clearheaded enough to see that the odds were against philosophy this time. He saw that it was hard to yoke love and wisdom. "In her magic presence," he confessed, "reason becomes ashamed of himself and wears the aspect of Pedantry or Calculation." What "if the Daemon of the man," he wisely speculated, "should throw him into circumstances favourable to the sentiment"? Then "reason would stand on a perilous, unsteady footing." Obviously, as far as Waldo Emerson was concerned, the circumstances already favored the sentiment. And though he went through his philosophical gestures, reminding himself how hard it was for a young man to determine the inner qualities of a beautiful woman and that the chances were she did not possess the virtues the lover valued in her, he seems to have come soon to the pleasing conclusion that, in this case at least, beauty was sufficient proof of goodness. The question of Ellen Tucker was, for him, as good as decided. He could detect "Nothing but light & oxygen" in New Hampshire.

Ellen herself, though she expected to have some financial means once she came into her share of the Tucker estate, was unrestrained by any calculating selfishness and, as Waldo later said, "shamed my ambition and prudence by her generous love in our first interview." Whether she went so far at their meetings in earlier months remains uncertain. It is certain that she did now. Some conversation of the sort remained fixed in the memory of her lover. "I described my prospects," he summarized it. "She said, I do not wish to hear of your prospects." He wrote more love poems in her album. In his own journal he was soon addressing Ellen in verses which gave the lie to the legend of emotional poverty he had been trying to attach to himself. "I am enamoured of thy loveliness," he wrote, "Lovesick with thy sweet beauty."

As Waldo lived one life and not two, he was doubtless un-abashed when he preached to Ellen's church a sermon he had recently written on the affections. It sounded as if it were intended for Ellen and himself. For him it served to restore the dignity of his philosophy, which had proved so unreliable in her presence. Love, he said, was a necessity; but it was not the body but the spiritual properties that we loved. The affections, he showed, with Plato's *Symposium* in mind no doubt, tended to expect perfection in the loved person, and from seeking perfection in the human friend were led to seek it in God.

By Christmas Eve he had returned to Cambridge and was an-nouncing the successful conclusion of his private mission. To his brother William he wrote that, having been "for one week engaged to Ellen Louisa Tucker a young lady who if you will trust my account is the fairest & best of her kind," he was "now as happy as it is safe in life to be." Ellen was, he explained, "the youngest daughter of the late Beza Tucker a merchant of Boston." During the residence of the Emersons in Roxbury they had known of the family whose home they passed as they followed the Dedham Turnpike into Boston. Ellen's mother had now been "three or four years the wife of Col W. A. Kent of Concord, N. H."

Waldo did not go farther into the family history of the Tuckers, which was heavy with misfortune and boded no good for Ellen. Her father, the prosperous merchant who had once been a pew-holder in the Reverend William Emerson's First Church in Boston and was later one of the founders of the Baptist Church in Rox-bury, died at the age of forty-eight. Five years later her brother,

George, a young medical student with leanings toward both literature and science, traveled abroad for his health and died at Paris,
doubtless of what he called "a horrid cold which has turn'd my
blood to melted lead." Her sister Mary died young. Now only her
sisters Margaret and Paulina and her mother, Mrs. Kent, survived.
Margaret was a victim of tuberculosis. It seems unlikely that either
of the lovers understood until after their engagement how seriously
Ellen's life was threatened by the same disease.

Back in Massachusetts, the minister resumed his supply preaching but kept in close touch with Ellen. He had hardly returned
home before he bought her a copy of a second gift book, *The
Offering,* edited, it seems, by Professor Andrews Norton as a
means of raising money for charity. Waldo himself had written
three of the anonymous contributions, two in verse and one in
prose. They were mere trifles he had salvaged from his journals
and notebooks. But a book with verse of his own was a fit gift
for Ellen, herself a poet.

His letters to Ellen were destroyed or are lost, but those of hers
which are still preserved prove that he was a faithful correspondent. She feared she would annoy him with "the metaphorical
droppings of a girl in her teens," and apparently she had the
humor to laugh at her own rhetorical sentimentalizing. It became
obvious that his old schoolmaster's instincts were still alive when
he put her to work reading a history of the Emperor Charles V,
doubtless Robertson's, and proposed writing to her in French.
She liked Charles V but had some difficulty in keeping her mind
on it. The proposed French letters would have caused both the
lovers some trouble. "I have been reviving some old French words
in my head," she wrote; "I find want of practice has put them
asleep but they walk drowsily forth and I doubt not I can catch
the idea of any thing you chuse to write. If it takes more of your
precious time to write in this way I would not." She loved to read
his "tinkling rhymes" but could not keep up with him in versify-

ing. "My muse," she said, "is a disobedient lady and loves not the
cold. . . . But you must weary of my feebly expressed thoughts—
which I am afraid are losing too much of their timidity. . . ."

The correspondence eventually ran to at least nearly forty letters
on her side. She humorously acknowledged his eight years' advantage in age and wisdom by calling him Grandpa and apologizing
for her own "half grown ideas." She admired his letters because
they were "not unmeaning love letters—written *only for courtship.*" After a few months she was doing French exercises for him
and even asking his help with her English compositions. Her ill-
nesses sometimes made her letters pathetic, but she generally kept
up her jaunty mood. She feared she was fading away and passing
him by in the journey of life in spite of his earlier start. At times
she was forced to put off his visits till she had better health, or
she was able to send him only brief notes. She wrote him love
poetry and wanted more from him.

The Emersons nearly all welcomed her. Her dislike of Andrew
Jackson showed that she was politically eligible as a member of
the family, but that was the least of her qualifications. When she
came to old Concord for a visit, Ruth Emerson thought her "a
blessing sent from heaven for Waldo" and she pleased Grandfather
Ripley, "the 'Apostle of half a century.' " There were a few grum-
blings from Aunt Mary, who had not yet seen her but whose eyes
seldom saw unmixed good.

For Waldo there was enough good fortune to make unfavorable
omens look unimportant. He was about to enter upon a regular
pastorate in spite of some suspicions on the part of the senior
minister who still nominally held it. Henry Ware had foreseen, no
doubt, that Waldo would be his colleague and successor at the
Second Church in Boston and had cautioned him against unor-
thodox tendencies. The young preacher made no humble apology.
"I have affected generally," he explained, "a mode of illustration
rather bolder than the usage of our preaching warrants, on the

principle that our religion is nothing limited or partial, but of universal application, & is interested in all that interests man." But Ware, whose large head gave an impression of stature belied by his puny frame, was not a serious obstacle. Though he had frigid manners and no deep enthusiasm, he was benevolent. "In calm hours and friendly company," said Waldo, "his face expanded into broad simple sunshine; and I thought *le bon Henri* a pumpkin-sweeting."

Certainly the exchange of opinion between the two men did not much affect opinion in the Second Church, which, in January, invited Waldo to become junior pastor. Out of seventy-nine persons voting, seventy-four were for him. He was to receive $1,200 a year, but it was agreed that after the end of Ware's connection, which would be soon, he would be advanced to the rank of pastor, with Ware's salary of $1,800. Waldo hesitated only because he feared that Ellen, whom he was already nursing through a severe attack of her dangerous malady, might need to travel for her health. Having got encouragement from her doctor, he decided to accept the offer.

Ignorant of the crisis in Ellen's health, Aunt Mary exploded with disgust at what she thought her nephew's vulgar success. She saw "no romance—all common, fat prosperity; not the poet, reckless of scholarship, glad to get his bread anyhow." She prophesied that he would "be as busy as a bee, yet as cautious as if he were a tailor making patterns." Aunt Mary gloried in her own vagabondage and poverty, and she very honestly took alarm at her nephew's prospect of marrying money. But within a few days she was contentedly setting herself up as schoolmistress to Ellen, whom she tutored by mail. She tried to prepare her to be, as she said, a lasting blessing to the man to whom it was her favored lot to be attached. She instructed her what religious books and what novels to read and ventured to hope that she did not paint or talk French.

To Waldo Emerson, now at Boston in the house of a Haskins
cousin in order to be near Ellen, prosperity did not seem real. At
the end of January, in "these times of tribulation," which he was
spending partly in Ellen's sick room as one of her nurses, he sent
his unenthusiastic acceptance to the Second Church. Ellen's ill
health must have been in his thoughts as he wrote: "I come to
you in weakness, and not in strength. In a short life, I have yet
had abundant experience of the uncertainty of human hopes." He
"cast many a lingering look around the walls" of 14 Divinity Hall,
a pleasant place to live. Two members of the Second Church were
ready to open their homes to him in Boston. He agreed to spend
the first month of his pastorate with George Sampson on North
Allen Street and afterwards to board with Abel Adams on Chardon
Street, not too long a walk from the church.

On Wednesday, the eleventh of March, 1829, the ordination
was like a family party. Edward and Charles and their mother and
Ellen's mother were witnesses. The family took pride in the new
pastor's "elegant & dignified" appearance and were moved to
tears by the honorable allusions made to his late father. Grandfather Ripley appeared "yet nobler in old age, like an oak that
gathers in venerableness what it loses in luxuriance." No eminent
preachers were present. Uncle Samuel Ripley preached the sermon; Grandfather Ripley gave the charge; Frothingham, pastor
of the Reverend William Emerson's old church, gave the right
hand of fellowship. Another of the ministers was Upham, Waldo's
college classmate. Gannett, a graduate of the year before Waldo's,
seemed endowed with prophetic vision as he addressed the members of the society, urging them to spare their pastor's strength,
to respect the independence of his ministry, and, even if he proved
too heterodox to suit them, to give him credit for courage at least.
They were not to hinder the preacher in his duty so long as they
could endure him at all; if they could not endure him, manner or

doctrine, they were to tell him so frankly and let him go. "If," said Gannett, "I must choose between the condition of a slave in Algiers, & the servitude of a clergyman, who dares not speak lest he shd startle a prejudice, give me the former."

Doubtless the ceremony was not too simple to suit Waldo. He heeded John Milton's warning that ordination had no mysterious virtue in it but was merely "the laying on of hands, an outward sign or symbol of admission," creating nothing and conferring nothing. After the ordination, the family joined the guests at the four long tables in the hall of the Hancock School, in the same street with the church. The ceremonies would hardly have been complete without some observance at the manse in Concord, and four pertinent lines on the wooden panel that had long served as a sort of Emerson album may well have been written there by Edward on this occasion:

> Holy & happy stand
> In consecrated gown
> Toil, till some angel hand
> Bring sleep & shroud & crown

To be pastor of the Second Church was an honor, and the salary substantial for a beginner. But the church, even if it was the second oldest in Boston, was no longer fashionable or wealthy. Its place of worship did not add to its attractiveness. The new junior pastor, unless he was completely preoccupied with his unaccustomed responsibilities as he walked along Hanover Street, must have marveled at the old but recently renovated edifice. It was so tall, with its three tiers of windows accenting its height, that it dwarfed the spire resting firmly but not very gracefully atop its large rectangular tower. The tower itself resembled a campanile built by mistake too close to the church. There were some unpleasant memories preserved in the stories told about the place. It had been called the Revenge Church because of its origin in a quarrel, and the

Cockerel Church because the figure of a cock had been perched upon its first weather vane, in derision, it is said, of the Reverend Peter Thacher, over whose ordination there had been fierce dissension. Tradition had it "that when the cock was placed upon the spindle, a merry fellow straddled over it and crowed three times to complete the ceremony."

Whether or not the new junior pastor was troubled by such old wives' tales, he could hardly have been unmindful of some somber figures in the past or present of his society. More than a century earlier the learned Puritan preachers Increase Mather and his son Cotton had both served the Second Church for many years. When Waldo climbed into the semicircular mahogany pulpit, he must have been painfully conscious of Henry Ware, Jr., still nominally his senior colleague. But when he faced the persons actually present, the pulpit's firm wings, extending laterally to make the semicircle into something resembling the Greek letter omega, and its dominating height, emphasized by the fluted columns that buttressed its curved front, doubtless gave him a sense of security. He had a psychological advantage that seemed to nullify the numerical superiority enjoyed by his congregation, which was broken up into little platoons sheltered only by the less formidable barriers of the pew walls and doors. Yet he needed courage, for he was a young man announcing new doctrines where the much respected senior pastor had recently repeated the articles of faith commonly accepted by Unitarians.

He seemed to be defiantly answering Ware's earlier admonitions when, in the first sermon he preached after being ordained, he charted his course, declaring that he intended henceforth to use a freedom befitting the greatness of the Gospel and its application to all human concerns. His own limitations were naturally strict enough, and it would be silly, he explained, to shut himself up within still narrower bounds. He would simply appeal to Biblical example if anybody complained about the want of sanctity in his style. He was willing to admit that the Scriptures were the direct voice of God. But he declared that the business of the church was to teach right living rather than religious dogma. In a second sermon he made it clear that he did not care to be an ecclesiastical policeman. He was still willing to keep up the ordinances of the church, but in the two sermons he gave notice that time-honored precedents were in danger.

He was soon averaging five introductory pastoral visits a day, and he felt them in every bone of his body. On his second Sunday he "preached at home all day & married a couple & baptized a child & assisted in the administration of the supper." He got hard-earned confidence. "I fear nothing now," he declared, "except the preparation of sermons. The prospect of one each week, for an indefinite time to come is almost terrifick." Exchanges with other pastors helped him, but there was no shirking the job of writing fresh sermons. Ellen was in Boston, at least much of the time, but he had to spend two or three hours a morning in writing and generally the whole afternoon in visiting. Charles, then living in the city, was struck by the increasingly eloquent preaching and by the amusing spectacle of the inexperienced pastor visiting his people "without any other guide or introduction, than his own knowledge of the street wherein they live." Sometimes Waldo "made long calls, kindly & affectionate on families who had no other claim to his attentions, than that of bearing the same name with his parishioners."

Even before the ordination at the Second Church, the radical schoolmaster Amos Bronson Alcott had listed Waldo Emerson as eleventh among the lesser preachers whose acquaintance he desired to make. A more enthusiastic hearer hazarded the opinion that "That young man will make another Channing." Undoubtedly many would have agreed with the New Bedford man who admired the young preacher's voice, "indefinite charm of simplicity and wisdom," and "occasional illustrations from nature" but found

"the fresh philosophical novelties" of the sermon hard to understand.

Ware more than once declared his satisfaction with what was
going on in his old pulpit, but actually he was first doubtful, then
deeply troubled. In answer to one of Ware's privately administered
admonitions, Waldo said he was distressed "that the idea sh'd
be given to my audience that I did not look to the Scriptures with
the same respect as others." He had only meant to say, he explained, "that my views of a preacher's duties were very high."
But the new preacher had reasoned out his course for years past
and was not blundering into strange heresies. Ware was broken-
hearted. The parish dwindled, he said tearfully, for the church was
afflicted with skepticism.

Doubtless it was the sermon that most appealed to the young
pastor, but it was only one of the nine parts of the order of exercises for both morning and afternoon as he once jotted them down:
prayer, Scriptures, hymn, prayer, hymn, sermon, prayer, hymn,
benediction. He halted in his prayers, ill at ease. He was fastidious
in his choice of words and hated stereotyped phrases. He complained that "the necessity of saying something & not stopping
abruptly led him to say what he would not have said—a kind of
insincerity." The ceaseless prayer, an aspiring and an actual living
toward ideals, which he had long since advised his hearers to
practice was something quite different from these public exercises.

As he himself had little music in him, most of the songs sung
by the choir or congregation must have given him as much pain
as the worst of them would have given to an expert. But he was
delighted by the singing of the peripatetic choir girl Charlotte
Cushman, afterward known in opera for her fine contralto voice
and later famous as an actress. Sometimes he was emotionally uplifted when the church was filled with voices as it was when
Charles Wesley's New Year's hymn was sung. That piece had
some resounding lines that his ear was not deaf to:

> Come, let us anew our journey pursue,
>   Roll round with the year,
> And never stand still till the Master appear!

What he cared for most in the hymns was the occasional bit of poetry he could detect and any evidences of liberal theology. In the old collection used in his church he was troubled by false theological views. There were, he considered, loose notions about immortality and gross conceptions of spiritual things. He put these opinions into a sermon and had a new hymnal adopted.

He found it awkward to visit sick people and mourners. Tales of his unhappy adventures among his parishioners got into circulation. Called to the deathbed of Captain Green, a rough-and-ready old Revolutionary officer who lived next door to the church, Waldo was diffident and embarrassed, fumbled among the clutter of things on the sick man's table, and began to talk about glassmaking. The captain was angry and told him that if he knew nothing to do at a deathbed but to lecture about glass bottles, he had better go. Another story told how Waldo, getting stuck in the middle of a prayer he was making at a funeral, took his hat and left without further ado. The young pastor himself might have jotted down many similar incidents of his professional life, no doubt, if he had been quick enough to realize the value of such trivia. But people shunned to record the circumstance which they best knew, he afterwards put it, "for example, the clergyman . . . his pecuniary and social and amiable or odious relations to his parish." It was only when you got far enough away from "these employments & meannesses" that their significance loomed larger and they appeared to be "the fit fable of which you are the moral."

In common with other preachers, Waldo Emerson was naturally discouraged when he thought of the mixed motives that brought his congregation to church. He already knew well enough, without putting it into so many words, that "Scarcely ten came to hear his sermon. But singing, or a new pelisse, or Cousin William, or the Sunday School, or a proprietors' meeting after church, or the merest anility in Hanover Street, were the beadles that brought and the bolts that hold his silent assembly in the church." Yet he wanted the opportunity of confronting even such a congregation. They were "fools," he admitted, but "potentially divine." He hoped to stick to his pulpit till it appeared that a better platform was available to him.

A few close friends meantime made his professional worries seem unimportant. Abel Adams, to whose house in Chardon Street Waldo moved his scanty belongings from George Sampson's home, was one of the most dependable and useful friends he ever had. Adams cared little for books but knew human nature and was a trusted adviser in financial matters. He exchanged Bibles with the young minister and they called themselves brothers. But Waldo had his mind mainly on Ellen. By the first of May she had left Boston and was hopefully traveling in the Connecticut Valley. Within a few weeks she had "fled like the Phenix bird" back to new Concord, and Waldo spent nearly all the latter half of June there, a part of the time in her sick room. She was "taken sick in the old way—very suddenly," and he concluded that "human happiness is very unstable." Back in Boston again that summer, he still hoped for her recovery and was thinking, it seems, of the possibility of settling with her in the peaceful corner of Roxbury where he had once lived.

Having returned to New Hampshire at the earliest possible moment, he set out with her on a long journey to improve her health. "Ellen & I came hither in a chaise this morng. an easy ride of 12 miles from Concord," he wrote to his brother Charles from the Shaker village of Canterbury. "Her mother followed us an hour or two later in coach with our fair & reverend baggage. Ellen bore the ride beautifully & if tomorrow shd. prove fair & she continues as well we mean to go on to Meredith bridge . . . or even possibly to Centre Harbor. . . . Mother Winkley or Sister Winkley hath given Ellen & I a long & earnest sermon on the 'beauty of virginity' & striven to dissuade us from our sinful purpose of 'living after the way of manhood & of womanhood in the earth' but I parried her persuasion & her denunciation as best I might & insisted we were yoked together by Heaven to provoke each other to good works so long as we lived. . . ."

Waldo, untouched by Mother Winkley's Shaker doctrines, entertained his pretty companion with a humorous rhyming journal of their progress. Her fortitude was tested by the journey. As they went on toward the White Mountains, they passed "thro much wind & some shower" and wished for a fire in August. But the open air seemed better for Ellen than her nurse and hot room at home. Waldo canceled his next Sunday's engagement with his church in Boston, and they turned westward to the Connecticut Valley before starting back to new Concord.

A few weeks later, in September, the lovers were off on another tour, this time from her home to the Merrimac River, on to Worcester, Springfield, and Hartford, and back through Worcester into New Hampshire. They carried half a dozen volumes of new novels besides some heavier reading. By day they rode in the chaise, while Mrs. Kent and her daughter Margaret came along in the carriage. At the taverns they read and scribbled. He preached a sermon or two in spite of a lame knee. They hurried northward on their return, as he wanted to get back to his own pulpit and Ellen doubtless needed to reach home a week or two before their wedding.

On the last day of the mouth, in her stepfather Colonel Kent's old mansion in the New Hampshire Concord, they were married. Charles, the only one of the groom's family at the wedding, had a great fondness for Waldo and did not live through "3 whole days in that big house full of women" without suffering a twinge of jealousy. Time was heavy on his hands "while W. & the fair Ellen were whispering honied words above stairs," as he said, "& I was

turned over to the compulsory attentions of the stranger folk."
But he managed to arouse himself to an effort at generosity.
"These lovers," he explained, "are blind—purblind these lovers
be—I forgive them freely." Early in October the married pair
were moving into the house of a Mrs. Hannah Keating, on, or
slightly off, Chardon Street, Boston, and close to the home of
Abel Adams. Waldo was soon laid up in his chair, unable to walk
without a cane. His sprained knee was now made worse by chronic
inflammation. On Sundays he preached sitting. He rode out with
Ellen every day when the weather was good.

His marriage had made him a man of some substance, or rather
had given him the promise of being so. "Men call me richer," he
put it, "I hope it will prove so—but shall be glad if the equipage
of the king & the queen for each hath their own doth not eat
up master Mammon on his quarter day." He settled down to his
new way of life. He bought a pair of dumbbells, doubtless in an
attempt to get exercise in spite of his lameness; deposited money in
the Globe Bank; paid Chickering $300 for a piano; subscribed to
the Boston Athenaeum; and bought books. As his knee got no
better, he quit his reputable doctors and hired a quack, who had
the good luck to cure him. He offered to pay $3 a week so that
Edward, now admitted to the bar and at work in New York with
William, could be kept from overwork; but he did not find his
own immediate financial prospects rosy. "I have a fancy," he
declared, "that if you shd examine my income & outlay since my
marriage you wd say I was poorer not richer, therefor. But richer
I surely am by all Ellen, if she bro't no penny."

In spite of his pastorate and his absorbing connection with Ellen
he was prepared, at least, to do a good deal of reading, perhaps
partly for his wife's benefit. In the year of his marriage he bought
copies of Montaigne, Rousseau, a Cooper novel, Scott's *Marmion,*
and Combe on the constitution of man. He borrowed Herder on
the philosophy of history, Marcus Aurelius, Plato, and a few other

authors from the Harvard College Library. He paid some small sums to the Boston Library Society and got good returns, borrowing such books as Xenophon on Socrates, Aristotle on ethics and politics, *Plutarch's Morals,* Lucretius, Epictetus, Beaumont and Fletcher, Massinger, Bishop Berkeley, Sir William Temple, Swift's *Gulliver's Travels, Clarissa Harlowe* and another novel of Richardson's, Erasmus Darwin's *Zoonomia,* Lamb's essays, Southey's *Thalaba,* Schiller's history of the Thirty Years' War, and Goethe's memoirs. He soon began to make heavy drafts upon the library of the Boston Athenaeum.

He was beginning a new and rewarding period of acquaintance with books. A few deftly turned phrases and philosophical distinctions such as he might borrow from a subtle mind like Coleridge's —talent and genius, fancy and imagination, reason and understanding—might help shape his old thoughts into a semblance of order. After years of nibbling at Coleridge, he suddenly became deeply interested in him that autumn and winter. In December he wrote Aunt Mary that he was reading *The Friend.* He was aware that she did not "speak of it with respect" but went on to inform her that "there are few or no books of pure literature so self-imprinting, that is so often remembered as Coleridge's." And a few days later he added a determined defense of his author. Early in the new year he sent William and Edward a list of books he was reading: "Coleridge's *Friend*—with great interest; Coleridge's 'Aids to Reflection' with yet deeper; Degerando *Hist. Comparée des Systemes de Philosophie,* I am beginning on the best recommendation. & one more book—the best Sermon I have read for some time, to wit, Combe's *Constitution of Man.* You see the present is too mighty for me, I cannot get away to do homage to the mighty past."

He debated books with his brothers and with Aunt Mary, an instigator or a severe critic of his thinking. Charles, by his own admission, was now "quite taken with Coleridge." Aunt Mary

sometimes professed to believe that Waldo did not value her and
would soon put her aside. She characteristically attacked him
obliquely by addressing Charles or some other member of the
family. "As to Waldo's letter," she once wrote, "say nothing to
him. It is time he should leave me. His sublime negations, his
non-informations, I have no right in the world to complain of."
Another letter showed that she was trying to keep up with the
philosophical Aunt Sarah Alden Ripley as well as with him, but
not very willingly. "Coleridge—& a few relations of his idealism,"
she grumbled, "I pick up & sit late & rise early to question of a
truth which can be of no consequence to me in the grave. Instead
of truth I might say illusion—sophistry. . . ." She was bewildered.
Her curiosity carried her along into new speculations, but she
looked with suspicion upon "the Kantian mania w'h has revived
within two or three years" and thought Kant and his followers as
destructive of theism as was Spinoza. She was sure she would
never part with her reasonably orthodox and reliable favorite
Doctor Samuel Clarke, but she saw that the newly popular philosophical doctrines left "the good old Clarke out of all reckoning."

Waldo bought a magnet, a frame for a view of Paestum, Bos-
well's *Life of Johnson,* a history of enthusiasm, the Boston Athenaeum catalogue, a subscription to the *Boston Daily Advertiser,*
a bird, a subscription to *The New Jerusalem Magazine,* another to
The Christian Examiner, another to *The North American Review,*
and another to *The Edinburgh Review.* Such things could probably come out of his own salary, but he undoubtedly could not
meet all his expenses from that restricted source. He sometimes
paid Mrs. Keating over $100 a month for the house, with board
it seems. In March, April, and May he had heavy expenses for
travel southward with Ellen, her sister Margaret going along
with them.

By the middle of March the three of them were in the Connecticut Valley again. At Hartford he preached three times in one Sun-

day. There he managed to bring Aunt Mary, who was apt to be
boarding about in odd places, for her first sight of Ellen. Ellen,
in the rhymed travel journal which it was her turn to keep on
this trip, recorded Aunt Mary's disappointment. As usual, however, Aunt Mary was not wholehearted in her verdict. "I like her
better better than I dreamt," she managed to bring out; and she
even discovered genius in the girl. But though she eventually declared that the young wife was "the lovliest Maddona of my
imajanation," she refused for the present to accept the usual estimate of Ellen's beauty.

On the whole the journey proved to be one more trial of endurance for Ellen. Sailing from New Haven, she and her sister
and Waldo encountered a gale that drove them into Norwalk
Roads for shelter. There they lay "pouting & snuffing the insuffer-
able mephitis of the cabin, & hearing the rain patter & looking
at each other grimly." There were "forty stout passengers . . .
sleeping or trying to sleep in an air that wd doubtless have put
out a lamp on the floor. But morning came, the wind abated, &
the steam chimney began once more to puff." After "a noble
passage up the Sound," during which they enjoyed the "fine sun
mild air, swift vessels, beautiful shores, noble seats," they got
to "this long London town" of New York.

There Waldo took over the doggerel journal from Ellen to in-
sert some satirical lines on the parades of splendid "paint, lace,
plumes, flowers, & brocades" on Broadway; but at the hotel she
found fit subjects for more of her own social satire. Amazed at
the brazenness of the city belles, she was, as she pictured herself,
the overmodest country lass, a

> wondering, eager, newcome clown
> And blushing like a country Miss
> To see the utter nakedness
> And how they cheat the legs of clothes
> While the long arms in state repose. . . .

But at last, safely on board the *Thistle,* she and Waldo were skirting Staten Island, then entering the muddy Raritan, the waterway to Philadelphia.

In that city, they left the U. S. Hotel for Sarah M'Elroy's boarding house, on the corner of Chestnut and Eleventh Streets. There Ellen discovered more grist for her metrical mill, but her habitual mood was far from satirical. William Furness, Waldo's boyhood friend and now a large part of Philadelphia for the young couple, "found them on one occasion walking with arms around each other, up & down their parlor." He was impressed by Ellen's youthfulness and delicacy. The young husband, he remembered, "borrowed my Hume's *Hist of England.*" But as Waldo was "Reluctant to inflict dry reading upon his child-wife, he said he would have her begin with the reign of Queen Eliz.ᵗʰ" He stayed over two Sundays, preached three sermons, and went with Ellen to see art treasures; but he soon became "sadly impatient" of the "petty engagements which tear time into slivers." By the first of April he was on his way home, leaving his wife with her sister Margaret in Philadelphia till, as he planned, he should return for them a few weeks later.

Before the end of May he and Ellen and Ruth Emerson were in Brookline, beginning their residence of several months in the ugly and old-fashioned but pleasant, comfortable Aspinwall house. To Charles, a frequent visitor there that summer, his mother seemed to have found a peaceful hermitage that agreed with her own serene soul. The unfortunate fact for Ellen was the cruel, inexorable chafing of the Massachusetts coast's east wind, which, she said, "blows blue & shrill." For her husband, a week of daily travel between Brookline and Boston was almost enough, but he was willing to sacrifice himself, or others, to her good. Except for a "universal benevolence," Charles observed, the young husband was "all called in & centred in Ellen." Charles, finding himself neglected, was hurt and wondered "whether t'is the invariable effect of business & marriage, to make one independent of, & therefore indifferent to old relationships & intimacies."

On Election Day in Boston, Waldo Emerson, chaplain of the state senate, sat comfortably in the pulpit and listened to Doctor Channing's "noble discourse." Waldo's selection as chaplain, in the summer of 1829, apparently had had no political significance, for the administration was Democratic Republican while he, with many other former Federalists, was presumably by that time at least nominally a National Republican. But probably he had had to acknowledge a definite affiliation with the National Republicans when, in the local election of the following December, he had been chosen to represent the fourth ward on the Boston school committee during the year 1830.

The committee meant a serious responsibility with little honor. Its twelve members were elected annually, one from each ward; and the mayor and aldermen belonged *ex officio*. The committee elected all the public-school teachers, determined salaries, and removed any teacher at discretion. Each of its regular subcommittees visited and watched over one of the city schools. Visitations, reports, quarterly meetings, special meetings, and informal conferences added up to a staggering total of hours for a conscientious member.

The young minister had been promptly assigned to the subcommittees on the Latin School and the Mayhew School. He was a graduate of the Latin School, and the Mayhew School was near his home. Except when he was out of town he seldom failed to do his part. During the year he served on a special committee to make the annual return of the Boston schools to the state, vainly tried to block changes in school regulations, wrote two quarterly reports for the subcommittee on the Mayhew School. It was discouraging business for him to generalize on hasty impressions of the work being done by the scholars. Once he reported that the subcommittee "spent the forenoon in the Reading Department.

. . . There was not an appearance of much diligence in the reading or spelling of this class. The first class read pretty well; had
advanced a little way in grammar; & were very well acquainted
with the map of the United States." Some divisions of the fourth
class, he faithfully recorded, were superior to the rest. One class
recited arithmetic extremely well, and there was good order in
the school. Such reports were tangible but not inspiring results
of many meetings and visitations. The Mayhew School was an
especially troublesome assignment because of an altercation over
disciplinary practices in vogue there.

In the manner of his father before him, Waldo Emerson resolved to be methodical. He wished that God would grant him
"persistency enough, so soon as I leave Brookline, and come to
my books, to do as I intend." He was trying to define his old
theory of self-reliance more sharply with the help of the Cole-
ridgean concept of reason, reason that was not reason but the
faculty by which one intuitively turned on, in one's inner self, the
current of divine will and idea. He thought he saw clearer light
on the seeming contradiction between self-reliance and God-
reliance. He paradoxically insisted "that the more exclusively
idiosyncratic a man is, the more general and infinite he is." God,
truth, shone directly into the soul, and "it is," he put it, "when
a man does not listen to himself, but to others, that he is de-
praved and misled."

In the autumn he was back in Chardon Street among his books,
but his meditations on such ideas were interrupted by some
speculations on a subject unhappily pressed upon his attention
by the ill health of his family. Was it "possible for religious principle to overcome the fear of death"? Bacon had listed what he
thought were passions and humors which could triumph over that
fear. Instances of defiance of death were familiar to everybody,
but were these instances of a conquest of the fear or merely of
success in setting it aside, mere want of thought? Even "spiritual

men" like Doctor Johnson frequently showed great apprehension and gloom at the thought of dissolution, Waldo recalled. Later he quoted Sir Thomas Browne's *Hydriotaphia* in his journal.

News came from New York that Edward seemed as much threatened by tuberculosis as Ellen and must travel. If he would not come to Boston and let his mother and Ellen nurse him, he ought to go to Magnolia in Florida, Waldo thought, rather than to the West Indian island of Santa Cruz, a more expensive and more restricted place. Florida still had the special attraction, Waldo supposed, of being Achille Murat's residence. "For my-self," he argued, "I would pay a hundred dollars to live a little while with Murat." When word came that Edward was about to sail southward alone, Ruth Emerson, having decided to make the voyage with him if he wanted her, hastily set out for New York but was delayed by head winds and arrived half an hour after he had sailed for Santa Cruz.

Ellen, taking her doctor's advice not to migrate to Cuba or else-where unless she was prepared to stay for ten years, decided to risk another winter in New England. If Edward's case was pathetic, Ellen's was more so and was a test of her husband's fortitude as well as of her own. The pathos came not only from her youth, her beauty, and her helplessness but also from what she and doubt-less Waldo believed to be her unfulfilled promise as a poet. On blank leaves in a diary which had once been her brother George's she had written some of her most revealing prose and verse. God, she said, had given her a harp, and she thought the strings were sound, though the bridge and frets were weak and wasting. She felt that every day she "ought to get one drop . . . of clear distilled essence" from her brain, but the drop did not come. Her moods fell or soared up suddenly. "Today," she once wrote, "my heart has been riding again on the south wind. . . ." Her fragile verses expressed her resignation or her constancy in a touching feminine manner. . . .

She kept on riding out day after day, believing that the open air gave her her chance for life. Before the end of January that chance had dwindled perceptibly, though Waldo was still hopeful. "As soon as the snows melt so as to give us passage," he said, "and as soon as she recovers her diminished strength so as to ride & walk we shall set out for Philad. or Baltimore, God helping us." She lived through another week of dying. But it seemed to those who were with her that they were witnessing a religious act in which there was not much room for pathos. When she was not torpid under the influence of opiates, she was serene. On the sixth of February Charles wrote that "her spirit seems winged for its flight. . . . Waldo is bowed down under the affliction, yet he says t'is like seeing an angel go to heaven." For Waldo's mother, full of piety and of affection for Ellen, "the closing scene of her short life" had "solemn & delightful interest." The girl was, she said, "calm & undismayed at the approach of death—& in a prayerful & resigned state of mind committed herself & all her dear friends unto God—biding each of us around her Farewell." On February 8, two hours after Ellen's death, Waldo wrote to Aunt Mary:

"My angel is gone to heaven this morning & I am alone in the world & strangely happy. Her lungs shall no more be torn nor her head scalded by her blood nor her whole life suffer from the warfare between the force & delicacy of her soul & the weakness of her frame. I said this morn & I do not know but it is true that I have never known a person in the world in whose separate existence as a soul I could so readily & fully believe . . . I see it plainly that things & duties will look coarse & vulgar enough to me when I find the romance of her presence (& romance is a beggarly word) withdrawn from them all. . . ."

Henry Ware preached the funeral sermon, and the nineteen-year-old Ellen, it seems, was buried according to her own request in her father's tomb in Roxbury. She had been the wife of Waldo Emerson less than a year and a half, yet she had stirred him more than anybody else ever had done or could do. Others of the family vied with him in praising her. Charles, who had known her exceptionally well, could not be eloquent enough about her. The image of Ellen that remained in his mind was, he said, "an Ideal that, if I were a Platonist, I should believe to have been one of the Forms of Beauty in the Universal Mind. She moved ever in an atmosphere of her own, a crystal sphere, & nothing vulgar in neighboring persons & circumstances touched her." Waldo himself wrote and rewrote her elegy in verse and prose. . . .

⭐

Emerson's Most Famous Speech

Let us go upon a literary pilgrimage. The shrine which we are to visit is sacred in the memory of scholars, although Mr. Howells, with dispassionate candor, once described it as the ugliest spot in the universe of God. It is Harvard Square. Eighty-six years ago —or, to be precise, on August 31, 1837, Phi Beta Kappa day—it was not without a certain tranquil, rural beauty. Great elms shadowed the little green, in whose center stood a town pump quite after the taste of Hawthorne—although very few Phi Beta Kappa men chose to utilize it on anniversary days, to the scandal of the water-drinking minority. Northwestward from the Square runs the broad road to Lexington and Concord, and on the left, opposite the low-fenced Harvard Yard, is the meetinghouse of the First Parish. This edifice, completed in 1834, was the successor of that log meetinghouse where just two hundred years before, in the summer of 1637, Anne Hutchinson had been brought to

---

The once-renowned Harvard professor and critic Bliss Perry takes the reader by the hand, unfortunately, as he describes the circumstances surrounding Emerson's remarkable address "The American Scholar." However, he makes the situation come alive. He gives us a sense of what it must have been like to sit listening to an Emerson who was full of promise but still only locally known. And he gives us an Emerson for today. This essay is abridged from Perry's *The Praise of Folly and Other Papers* (1923) and is reprinted with the permission of the Houghton Mifflin Company.

52

trial by the New England Theocracy, and condemned to exile. If any ghosts of the past are hovering in the First Parish Church on this August morning of 1837, surely among them is the amused ghost of that clever woman, waiting to see what will happen to a new champion of rebellion.

Here, then, is our shrine, a plain wooden meetinghouse in a country village, built big enough for the modest needs of Harvard University on its anniversary occasions. Let us march toward it in the procession of our Phi Beta Kappa brethren, two hundred and fifteen strong, starting at twelve o'clock precisely from University Hall, in the middle of the Harvard Yard. Preceded by a band of music and the dark-gowned undergraduate members, the black-coated double file of graduate members emerge from the Yard, cross the road—the dust has been laid by the unwonted rain of the previous day—and halt in front of the meetinghouse. The undergraduates open to the right and left, and the President of Phi Beta Kappa, the secretary, chaplain, orator, and poet enter in that order, followed by the members, two and two, according to seniority. Brother John Pierce, D.D., of Brookline (Harvard, 1793), indefatigable attendant and notetaker of Harvard anniversaries, will describe the occasion—an epoch-making occasion, although he did not suspect it. . . .

And now the music of the brass band blares out into silence at last, and the great audience hushes itself. The Reverend Mr. Rogers of Boston offers a prayer which wins the full approval of Brother Pierce, being "singularly devout, short, and appropriate." Then, introduced by the President of the Society, rises the speaker of the day.

Let us look at him as he was then—and with the eyes of that audience—not as we know him now in marble and bronze, gleaming with the serene light of earthly immortality. He is a tall, thin man of thirty-four, with sloping shoulders, a man born, you would say, like his ancestors for seven generations, to wear black. His

face is asymmetrical. Seen from one side, it is that of a shrewd
New England farmer; from the other, it is a face of a seer, a

> Prophetic soul of the wide world
> Dreaming on things to come.

The cheeks are fresh-colored, like those of all the Emersons. The
thin hair is brown. The eyes are deep blue, with violet lights. He
stoops a trifle as he arranges his manuscript upon the pulpit. His
manner, though slightly constrained, is suave and courteous. No
one in that church, as the Reverend Mr. Emerson pronounces
the conventional words "Mr. President and Gentlemen," doubts
for a moment his ability to deliver an acceptable discourse. Indeed, he had delivered the Phi Beta Kappa poem, three years before. He belonged, as Dr. Holmes said afterward, to the academic races. This is no amateur, but a professional. . . .

I do not say that he won everybody in that packed meetinghouse. Certainly he did not convince our hard-headed Brother
John Pierce, sitting there on a front seat immovable and uncon-
vincible—watch in hand. Listen to his impression of the address;
but listen respectfully, for he is an honest man, and he utters the
verdict of the older generation:

Rev. Ralph Waldo Emerson gave an oration, of 1¼ hour, on "The
American Scholar." It was to me in the misty, dreamy, unintelligible
style of Swedenborg, Coleridge, and Carlyle. He professed to have
method; but I could not trace it, except in his own annunciation. It was
well spoken, and all seemed to attend, but how many were in my own
predicament of making little of it I have no means of ascertaining.
Toward the close, and indeed in many parts of his discourse, he spoke
severely of our dependence on British literature. Notwithstanding, I
much question whether he himself would have written such an apparently incoherent and unintelligible address, had he not been familiar
with the writings of the authors above named. He had already, in
1834, delivered a poem before the Society.

And now farewell to Brother Pierce—though he lives to attend eleven more meetings of the Society. The good man had his chance, too!

I must call three other witnesses to the effect of the oration, familiar to many of you as their testimony may be. Let us hear first a clever young Boston doctor, son of the minister of the First Church in Cambridge and brought up in its gambrel-roofed parsonage. He was the pet and the glory of the class of 1829. He had delighted the Phi Beta Kappa Society with his poem in 1836. He is not yet the "Autocrat," but he knows his own mind and the mind of the younger generation. Oliver Wendell Holmes testifies:

This grand Oration was our intellectual Declaration of Independence. Nothing like it had been heard in the halls of Harvard since Samuel Adams supported the affirmative of the question, "Whether it be lawful to resist the chief magistrate, if the commonwealth cannot otherwise be preserved." It was easy to find fault with an expression here and there. The dignity, not to say the formality of an Academic assembly was startled by the realism that looked for the infinite in "the meal in the firkin; the milk in the pan." They could understand the deep thoughts suggested by "the meanest flower that blows," but these domestic illustrations had a kind of nursery homeliness about them which the grave professors and sedate clergymen were unused to expect on so stately an occasion. But the young men went out from it as if a prophet had been proclaiming to them "Thus saith the Lord." No listener ever forgot that Address, and among all the noble utterances of the speaker it may be questioned if one ever contained more truth in language more like that of immediate inspiration. . . .

Let us next call to the witness stand that other Cambridge boy . . . in the audience—the reckless, irreverent "Jamie" Lowell of 1837; sober enough now, when he gives his testimony, and it is the testimony, you will remember, of one of the few genuine critics whom America has produced:

The Puritan revolt had made us ecclesiastically and the Revolution politically independent, but we were socially and intellectually moored to English thought, till Emerson cut the cable and gave us a chance at the dangers and glories of blue water. No man young enough to have felt it can forget or cease to be grateful for the mental and moral *nudge* which he received from the writings of his high-minded and brave-spirited countryman. . . . His oration before the Phi Beta Kappa Society at Cambridge, some thirty years ago, was an event without any former parallel in our literary annals, a scene to be always treasured in the memory for its picturesqueness and its inspiration. What crowded and breathless aisles, what windows clustering with eager heads, what enthusiasm of approval, what grim silence of foregone dissent! It was our Yankee version of a lecture by Abélard, our Harvard parallel to the last public appearances of Schelling. . . .

Finally, lest you may think that the mere spell of the orator's spoken word charmed such hearers as Holmes and Lowell into an unreasoning discipleship, listen to an opinion from across the water, by a Scotchman who called no man, save Goethe, master, and who read Emerson's speech in the vast solitude of London town. Thomas Carlyle wrote:

My friend! You know not what you have done for me there. It was long decades of years that I heard nothing but the infinite jangling and jabbering, and inarticulate twittering and screeching, and my soul had sunk down sorrowful, and said there is no articulate speaking then any more, and thou art solitary among stranger-creatures? and lo, out of the West comes a clear utterance, clearly recognizable as a *man's* voice, and I *have* a kinsman and brother: God be thanked for it! I could have *wept* to read that speech; the clear high melody of it went tingling through my heart; I said to my wife, "There, woman!" She read; and returned, and charges me to return for answer, "that there has been nothing met with like it since Schiller went silent." My brave Emerson! And all this has been lying silent, quite tranquil in him, these seven years, and the "vociferous platitude," dinning his ears on all sides, and he quietly answering no word; and a whole world of Thought has silently built itself in these calm depths, and, the day being come, says quite softly, as if it were a common thing, "Yes, I *am* here too." Miss

Martineau tells me, "Some say it is inspired, some say it is mad." Exactly so; no *say* could be suitabler. But for you, my dear friend, I say and pray heartily: may God grant you strength; for you have a *fearful* work to do! Fearful I call it; and yet it is great, and the greatest.

Many readers still imagine that Emerson's address had the advantage of a new theme. It did not. His subject, "The American Scholar," had been a conventional theme of Phi Beta Kappa orations ever since he was a boy. The records of the Harvard Chapter prove this fact, beyond dispute. . . .

You will thus perceive that when the Reverend R. W. Emerson announced in 1837 that his subject was to be "The American Scholar," the Cambridge audience could settle back comfortably in their seats, knowing pretty well what was coming—as you and I do when we listen to a Christmas or an Easter sermon. And I do not need to add that the comfortable Cambridge audience guessed wrong.

What was it, after all, that Emerson said, upon his hackneyed theme? What was it that puzzled the elders, and entranced the youth, and sowed the seeds of division? At the Phi Beta Kappa dinner in University Hall, following the exercises in the church—a dinner too Bacchanalian, alas, for the taste of Brother John Pierce —Emerson was toasted in these words: "Mr. President, I suppose you all know where the orator came from; and I suppose all know what he said. I give you—the Spirit of Concord—*it makes us all of one mind.*" The pun was clever enough—as Phi Beta Kappa dinners go—but the well-meant compliment went very wide of the truth. Far from making them all of one mind, the man from Concord had sowed discord—and Emerson, at least, knew it. At the Phi Beta Kappa dinner of the next year, he is aware, his *Journal* tells us, of the "averted faces," and the aversion dated from this very thirty-first of August, 1837—it had only ripened by the summer of 1838 and the "Divinity School Address." What had he really uttered in this speech, which was no loving cup, but a sword?

He had begun with decorous sentences, quiet and clear as the daylight. His very subject, he admits, is prescribed by the occasion. But before one knows it, he is making his first distinction, namely, that Man, in being divided into Men, has suffered, has become a thing—a farmer, let us say, instead of Man on the farm. Now the Scholar should be *Man Thinking,* not a mere thinker, or, still worse, the parrot of other men's thinking. What are the influences which the scholar receives?

There are three main influences: Nature, the Past—typified by Books—and Action.

First, then, Nature. "Every day, the sun; and, after sunset, Night and her stars. Ever the winds blow; ever the grass grows." But the scholar must ask what all this means. What *is* Nature? And then comes the puzzling Emersonian answer, already expressed in that little blue-covered unsold book of the year: Nature is the opposite of the soul, answering to it part for part. (I can fancy Brother John Pierce looking at his watch. Ten minutes gone, and is this nonsense about Nature, what we came into the meeting-house to hear?)

But the orator, after these cryptic paragraphs about Nature, is already touching the second influence upon the spirit of the scholar —namely, the Past, or, let us say for convenience, Books. (I imagine that Brother Pierce looks relieved. Books? He has been hearing Phi Beta Kappa talk about books for forty years. It is a safe subject. And yet what is it that the minister from Concord seems to be saying now?) The theory of books is noble, but each age must write its own books. It is the act of creation that is sacred, not the record. The poet chanting was felt to be a divine man: henceforth the chant is divine also. Instantly the book becomes noxious; the guide is a tyrant, though colleges are built on it. (Can he mean the Bible, wonders Professor Ware? Yes, Professor

Ware, he does mean the Bible, and he will say so in your own Divinity School upon the invitation of your own students, on the fifteenth of July next! Listen to him as he goes on!) The one thing in the world, of value, is the active soul. The book, the college, the institution of any kind, stop with some past utterance of genius. This is good, say they—let us hold by this. *They pin me down.* They look backward and not forward. Books are for the scholar's idle times. They serve us best when they aim, not to drill, but to create—when they set the hearts of youth on flame. (I should like to watch Professor Ned Channing's sarcastic face, as Waldo Emerson proclaims this doctrine: Waldo Emerson, who had proved himself in college neither drillable nor inflammable!)

But the imperturbable orator of the day has now reached the third section of his address—a plea for Action. Remember that we are in the golden and serious age of American Rhetoric, and do not smile when Emerson argues that action enriches the scholar's vocabulary! It is pearls and rubies to his discourse! Life is our dictionary. But action is after all better than books. Character is higher than intellect. Thinking is a partial act. The scholar loses no hour which the man lives. Labor is sacred. There is virtue yet in the hoe and the spade even in unlearned hands. (I catch grave young Henry Thoreau smiling a little as Mr. Emerson utters this wholesome New England doctrine of manual labor—for he has watched the minister trying to spade his new Concord garden, and making but a sorry job of it!)

It remains, concludes the speaker, to say something of the scholar's duties. They may all be comprised in self-trust. Let him not quit his belief that a popgun is a popgun, though the ancient and honorable of the earth affirm it to be the crack of doom. Let him be free and brave. The world is still fluid, still alive. *Men* count—not "the mass"—"the herd." The private life is the true kingdom. Act for yourself: the man has never lived that can feed us ever. (Professor Ware—stout old war-horse—pricks up his ears

again!) But now the orator is sweeping on to his climax: This age
of Revolution in which we are living is a very good age. Accept it:
embrace the common, the familiar, the low. Burns and Wordsworth and Carlyle are right. Give me insight into today, and you
may have the antique and future worlds. The important thing is
the *single person. The man is all.*

Then follows the wonderful peroration, which you would never
forgive me for not quoting word for word:

. . . Mr. President and Gentlemen, this confidence in the unsearched
might of man belongs, by all motives, by all prophecy, by all preparation, to the American Scholar. We have listened too long to the courtly
muses of Europe. The spirit of the American freeman is already suspected to be timid, imitative, tame: Public and private avarice make the
air we breathe thick and fat. The scholar is decent, indolent, complaisant. See already the tragic consequence. The mind of this country,
taught to aim at low objects, eats upon itself. There is no work for any
but the decorous and the complaisant. Young men of the fairest promise, who begin life upon our shores, inflated by the mountain winds,
shined upon by all the stars of God, find the earth below not in unison
with these, but are hindered from action by the disgust which the principles on which business is managed inspire, and turn drudges, or die of
disgust, some of them suicides. What is the remedy? They did not yet
see, and thousands of young men as hopeful now crowding to the barriers for the career do not yet see, that if the single man plant himself
indomitably on his instincts, and there abide, the huge world will come
round to him. Patience—patience; with the shades of all the good and
great for company; and for solace the perspective of your own infinite
life; and for work the study and the communication of principles, the
making those instincts prevalent, the conversion of the world. Is it not
the chief disgrace in the world, not to be an unit—not to be reckoned
one character—not to yield that peculiar fruit which each man was
created to bear, but to be reckoned in the gross, in the hundred, or the
thousand, of the party, the section, to which we belong; and our opinion
predicted geographically, as the north, or the south? Not so, brothers
and friends—please God, ours shall not be so. We will walk on our own
feet; we will work with our own hands; we will speak our own minds.
The study of letters shall be no longer a name for pity, for doubt, and

for sensual indulgence. The dread of man and the love of man shall be a wall of defense and a wreath of joy around all. A nation of men will for the first time exist, because each believes himself inspired by the Divine Soul which also inspires all men.

That, then, is what Emerson said, eighty-six years ago. What do we think of it? We know what Brother Pierce thought of it, and what was the verdict of Holmes and Lowell and Carlyle. I have amused myself—though I may have wearied you—by intimating what this hearer and that, among the long-vanished audience, may have surmised or hoped or resolved in his own heart, as those beautiful cadences ceased at last, and the great hour was over. I might tell what was said in the newspapers and in the reviews, and how the entire edition of the address was sold out in one month, whereas it took thirteen years to sell the first five hundred copies of the orator's book on *Nature*. Yet all such evidence, interesting as it may be to one's antiquarian curiosity, does not fully explain the meaning or the power of Emerson's address.

The words of Emerson's speech are still legible upon the printed page, but how small a portion of any speech are the mere words! Boys declaim them in school, "meek young men in libraries" study the sources, literary historians endeavor to reconstruct the time and place of utterance. Yet the magic has fled with the magical hour, and the words seem only the garments of a soul that has escaped. The chemical formula for a great speech seems simple enough, but it is mysterious, like all simple things; it is *a Man plus the atmosphere of a given epoch*. The speech falls flat if it be uttered a year, a month, a day earlier or later than its appointed hour. See young Wendell Phillips fighting his way to the platform of Faneuil Hall on December 8 of that very year, 1837, to defend the memory of Lovejoy from the attack of the Attorney General of Massachusetts. It is now or never for what Phillips has to say, and Phillips knows it. See him forty-four years later, in Sanders

Theater, as the Phi Beta Kappa orator of 1881, defending Russian Nihilism; some of us can remember the tense excitement of the American public in that hour over the question of freedom in Russia. Almost no one in Sanders Theater knew what Phillips was to say. Official Harvard, as always, distrusted him. His flashing eloquence, that noon, was the electric discharge, through him, of forces greater than the orator. If you will read that address of 1881 today, you cannot withhold your admiration for the cunning art of the consummate craftsman. The right words are all there in their right places. But the spell is broken; "the image of the God is gone."

Now, it is a part of the genius and the glory of Emerson that his spoken words have the accent of literature. Their specific form is, indeed, shaped by the heat and pressure of an occasion. But their substance is perdurable. His phrases are final phrases. His aim is Truth, and not mere eloquence. He has, indeed, learned the art of rhetoric from Everett and Webster, but he has also learned, by watching them, to distrust rhetoric—to keep it in its place. He would like to win his immediate audience, no doubt, but he is forever saying to himself, as Lincoln said of his debates with Douglas in 1858, "there is bigger game than this." Lincoln's ultimate object was to justify the fundamental principles of free government. Emerson's goal was the Truth that sets men free. His words are literature because the Truth that he perceived could be revealed only through Beauty. The revealing phrase is lovely, and the uncovered face of Truth is lovelier still. As Emerson discourses of Nature and Books and Action, he lays bare his own mind, as an athlete strips himself for the race. Exquisite perception of external beauty, ripened wisdom, high courage—these were the man, and by their perfect expression of the man's qualities Emerson's addresses win their place as literature. We read them today as we read Montaigne or Bacon, as something forever alive.

I remarked to a friend the other day that I was trying to imagine what Emerson would say if he had to make his Phi Beta Kappa speech over again in the present hour. "If Emerson were living to-day," was the reply, "he would be a very different Emerson." In one sense, of course, my friend was right. If Emerson had been born seventy-five years later, he would have read Tolstoy and Ibsen, he would have studied under William James, and he would use a somewhat different vocabulary. It is likely that he would have written no *Journals.* He would have missed the discipline and sup-port of the Lyceum audiences. But he would certainly be giving Lowell Institute lectures, as of old, and writing for the *Atlantic Monthly,* and lunching with the Saturday Club. It is certain that he would be making Phi Beta Kappa speeches, and I think we may be allowed to guess what he would say. He would still, I be-lieve, have a message for you and me, a message for our academic communities, and a counsel of perfection for the United States.

To the private person he would announce, with the old serenity: "The sun shines today also"—"and, after sunset, Night and her stars." In uttering this gospel of Nature he would use new terms, for his mind would have been fascinated by the new discoveries. But while the illustrations would be novel, he would still assert the universality of Law. He would still say: Books are good, but the living soul is better. "Do not teach me out of Leibnitz and Schel-ling, and I shall find it all out myself." He would still preach to us the gospel of the will, or, in William James's phrase, "the will to believe." "When you renounce your early visions, then dies the man in you." Be a unit. In this whirring social machinery of the twentieth century, in this over-organized, sentimentalized, and easily stampeded age, possess your own soul. By and by the snow-storm of illusions will cease, and you will be left alone with the moral laws of the universe, you alone and they alone. When that supreme hour comes, meet it without fear.

Emerson's message to the academic community would have, I think, a note of yearning. The historic Emerson always wished to be one of us. There was no time in his long career, his biographer says, when he would not gladly have accepted a professorship of rhetoric in any college. If he were of our generation, but still, as of old, outside of our own immediate circle, would he not say: "O you who are cramped in costly buildings, clogged with routine, preoccupied with administrative machinery, how can you see the sun whether it be shining? Where is your free hour for Night and her stars? You are learned in bibliographies, expert in card catalogues, masters of a thousand specialties. You are documented, certificated, sophisticated. But have you the old eager reverence for the great books? And where, by the way, are your own books? From these thousands of American colleges and universities, how many vital, creative books are born? The university of Walden Pond had 'Whim' written above its doorposts, but it bred literature. There was once a type of productive scholar who may be described as 'he that scattereth, and yet increaseth,' but your amazing and multifarious activity, is not much of it wastage rather than growth? Simplify! Coordinate! Find yourselves, and then lift up your hearts!"

And finally I am sure that the spirit of Emerson, if he were revisiting this "great sensual avaricious America," as the historic Emerson once called it, would have a message for the United States in this hour of cowardice, disillusionment, and inhibition. Unless Emerson came back from the underworld with a changed soul, he would assert the supremacy of moral obligations. He would perceive, as in his lifetime, that a "diffidence in the soul was creeping over the American mind." But he would shame that diffidence. He would rally the distrustful. Can we not hear once more his clear and quiet voice: The gods are forever in their places: first, Righteousness, Justice, and Liberty, and after these, Fellowship and Peace. The Law holds. The foundations of human society are moral foundations. They cannot be shaken, even though whole empires should lose their senses and debauch their souls and go toppling down. Be steady. "This time, like all times, is a very good one, if we but know what to do with it." Behold the Law: "God is, not was; He speaketh, not spake." The world is very wide, very strange, it terrifies us, it seems plunging from its orbit. But it cannot plunge from its orbit; that was fixed before the foundation of the world. Patience—patience. Our earth is whirling on its way from God and to God, and the law of its being is the same law of obedience and of faith which is written in the heart of the obscurest scholar.

⊗

Emerson at Sea

It was 1847, the year before the year of revolutions. Emerson was forty-four, and a new occasion had presented itself for extending his travels across the sea. For some time he had felt the need of a special stimulus; he had reached one of those dead points when the stars stand still in one's inward firmament and one requires some foreign force to prevent stagnation. His energies had ebbed, he had no thoughts, and America had come to seem of a village littleness. And now the Mechanics' Institutes, rising through the North of England, were urging him to come and lecture to them. Carlyle was urging him, too. Why shouldn't he go?

"In March, many weathers"; and in life many. He had often looked with longing eyes toward Europe. He had had his dreams of living there, perverse dreams, he felt, but very inspiriting. He

Here we have Emerson at an important point in his life. He needs to cross the ocean, to encounter again the bright British minds which have been so stimulating to him. He needs psychic as well as physical distance from America, and he has not been abroad for over a decade. Brooks pictures Emerson's state of mind and then the effects of his travel. The chapter is animated by the enthusiasm that made Brooks one of the main popularizers of nineteenth-century American literature. The style is flowing, personal. The chapter, untitled in the source, is abridged from the book *The Life of Emerson* by Van Wyck Brooks. Copyright, 1932, by E. P. Dutton & Co., Inc. Renewal, ©, 1960 by Van Wyck Brooks. Reprinted by permission of the publishers.

had dreamed of Valencia, Florence, Rome, Berlin, but of Oxford and Cambridge especially; he had read with the frankest envy Aubrey's anecdotes and the letters of English scholars. Their life was a complete circle of means and ends; and they had an audience, no poor, scattered following like his own, no mere handful of uncritical men and women, but a dense, compact body of instructed minds. What precise, what powerful demands were made upon them, and how these demands stirred them to labor and concentration! If he languished himself at times, if his thought remained so often vague and cloudy, was it not because so little was expected of him? The needs he addressed were so very far from conscious; he felt no sort of teamwork between himself and his listeners. (What was it the old lady said, that she never understood a word he uttered?—but she liked to go and see him just the same, standing up on the platform, looking as if he thought everybody else was just as good as he was. Pleasant enough, but not exactly stimulating. If she had only been able to catechize him a little, make him define his ideas, he would not have been quite so much "up in the air.") It was very hard to go beyond your public. If they were satisfied with your poor performance, you could scarcely make it better. But when they recognized what was good and delighted in it, you aspired and burned and toiled till you achieved it.

Yes, he had envied the thinkers of England, the richness, the calm assiduity, unhasting, unresting, of their lives. (Eupeptic studying-mills, cast-iron men, whose powers of endurance compared with those of the Americans as the steam hammer with the music box.) Their lot could never be his, but he envied it none the less—in hours like these. When his own tide was in flood it was easy to feel that his duty was at home: he could well defy these lingering looks *behind*. But when the tide ebbed, toward evening, on rainy days—that was another story. In America the people meant that men of thought should be ornamental merely. There was Everett, for instance, with his Liberty and his Dying

Demosthenes, and in practice wearing the slaveholder's whip in his buttonhole; and Eliot with his *History of Liberty* and his votes for South Carolina; and Sparks and Felton, who carried Demosthenes clean for slavery. Bancroft, Emerson said to himself, would never have known George Fox had he met him on the street, the same George Fox he had eulogized so well. (Historical democrats, all these men, interested in dead or organized, but not in organizing, freedom.) Was it true that deep convictions, realistic visions of a more enlightened society, were not to be entertained by a race that was busily settling a continent? They were pretty souls, these American men of thought; they gave such a fillip to the emotions on the Fourth of July! And they slept away the rest of their days, becalmed. No strong wind filled their sails, and they lost their incentive. For no commanding cry came from the void. . . .

Alas for America! An air loaded with poppy, and all running to leaves, to suckers, to tendrils, to miscellany, dispersion and sloth. A wilderness of capabilities, of a many-turning, Ulyssean culture; an irresistibility like Nature's, and, like Nature, without conscience. Everything speedy, everything new and slight. Shingle palaces, shingle cities, picnic universities. Leather not tanned; sulphuric acid, half-strength; knees, instead of grand old oak, sawed out of refuse sapling; for stone, well-sanded pumpkin-pine! An art scarcely more than the national taste for whittling: no independent creation of the sort that requires an artist charged in his single head with a nation's force. And hearts too soon despondent. Young men, young women, at thirty and even earlier losing all spring and vivacity: let them fail in their first undertaking, and the rest was rock and shallow.

Emerson had other moods. If now, as so often before, his estimate of America was low, it rose again as often to heroic proportions. He had felt so many times the greatness of his opportunity. It was something to be the Hesiod of a dawning nation, the Ennius, the Venerable Bede, up so early before the break of day. But the country seemed sadly naked in these hours of depression, naked, unatmospheric. Boston was mean and petty beside life in Concord, and Concord was so limited, so lonely, so insular! Pathetic was the sight of Edmund Hosmer creeping into one's barn, just on the chance of a little conversation. It was true he had often scoffed at travel—as if there were any country where they did not scald the milk-pans and burn the brushwood! As if every traveler were not a mere impertinence when he came among the diligent in their places! As if one could ever hope to find in geography the ailment the mind was seeking! A foolish American passion, this running about in the hotels and theaters of Europe.

He still scoffed at travel. A mark, this gadding abroad, this European complaint, of youth, of an endless novitiate, a proof that America was not ripe for the reign of heroic instincts. What could any one expect of travel but confirmation of his simplest sentiments at home? Still, even this, at the moment, might have its value; and he wanted a bath in the currents of the world's thought. There were facts of science he could only obtain in England, new theories which, for want of a learned class at home, he had never heard of till years after they were published. And he wanted to know the greatest of his contemporaries, know them not merely through books: at a spoken word, at the touch of a hand, a whole new view of the world passed into one's mind like lightning. He would see his own society in relief, in contrast with other societies; he would see the utmost that social man had accomplished—an aristocratic system with as few abatements as possible—model men, the distinctions that were flouted too easily at home. Above all, the scholars, the mighty workers of England: he would meet these giants and measure himself beside them. (And find an audience, too, the most exacting, one that would rouse and frighten him.) Carlyle was undoubtedly right. He would get an "immense quantity of food for ideas."

Carlyle! What wealth of being that name signified! How the

sight of that man's handwriting had always warmed his heart at the Post Office window! A redeemer of life, Carlyle, seeking no reward, warping his genius to no dull public, writing for he knew not whom and finding his readers at last in the valley of the Mississippi—readers who brooded on the pictures he had painted, untwisted the many-colored meanings which he had spun and woven into so rich a web of sentences, domesticated in so many remotest heads the humor, philosophy, learning, which, year by year, in summer and in frost, this lonely man had lived in the moors of Scotland! A true man of letters, Emerson said to himself, one who made good the place and function of Erasmus, of Dryden, Johnson, Swift, to one's own generation, who sustained the dignity of his profession of author in England. It was true that he mixed himself a little too much with his erring and grieving nations and saddened the picture. Health belonged to the author, too, Goethean health and cheerfulness! And his aims were sometimes paltry; he would draw weapons from the skies to fight for some wretched English monopoly or prejudice. And the slam-bang style, that grotesque, apocalyptic strain, was far from the Periclean. (O Carlyle, the merit of glass is not to be seen, but to be seen through; and every crystal and lamina of your glass is visible!) But what rules for the illumination of windows could ever apply to the Aurora Borealis? And what life he endowed the world with, this worshipper of strength, heedless much whether its present phase were divine or diabolic! He scorned all paper formulas, all "Pantheism, Pot-theism, Mydoxy, Thydoxy." ("Did the upholsterers make this Universe? Were you created by the Tailor?") And right he was in believing that every noble creature contained, if savage passions, also fit checks and grand impulses within him, and had his own resources, and however erring would return from far.

Again and again Emerson had sent his friends to that king's house in Chelsea—Alcott, Margaret Fuller, Henry James, Hedge, Theodore Parker, that the best of America might meet the best of

England. The shrewdest comments had come back from the lover of heroes, shrewd, humorous, benign: "The good Alcott, with his long, lean face and figure, with his grey, worn temples and mild, radiant eyes, all bent on saving the world by a return to acorns and the golden age. . . . A kind of venerable Don Quixote, whom nobody can even laugh at without loving! . . . Let him love me as he can, and live on vegetables in peace; as I, living *partly* on vegetables, will continue to love him! . . . Margaret Fuller: a true heroic mind, altogether unique, so far as I know, among the writing women of this generation. . . . Such a predetermination to *eat* this big universe as her oyster or her egg, and to be absolute empress of all height and glory in it that her heart could conceive, I have not before seen in any human soul. Her 'mountain *me*' indeed:—but her courage too is high and clear, her chivalrous nobleness indeed is great; her veracity, in its deepest sense, *à toute épreuve*. . . . Theodore Parker, a most hardy, compact, clever little fellow, full of decisive utterance, with humor and good humor, shining like a sun amid multitudes of watery comets and tenebrific constellations, too sorrowful without such admixture on occasion! . . . Frederic Hedge, one of the sturdiest little fellows I have come across for many a day. A face like a rock, a voice like a howitzer; only his honest kind grey eyes reassure you a little." A joy to have one's friends seen by such eyes, eyes that had seen Daniel Webster, too: "That amorphous craglike face; the dull black eyes under their precipice of brows, like dull anthracite furnaces, needing only to be *blown;* the mastiff mouth accurately closed:—I have not traced as much of *silent berserker-rage,* that I remember of, in any other man." A joy to have those thirsty eyes of Carlyle, those portrait-eating, portrait-painting eyes, fall full on the great forehead one had followed about in one's youth from courthouse to Senate! And now Carlyle had fixed his eyes upon *him.* "Come if you dare," he had written; "I said there was a room, house-room and heart-room, constantly waiting you here, and you shall see blockheads by the million. *Pickwick* himself shall be visible; innocent young Dickens reserved for a questionable fate. The great Wordsworth shall talk till you yourself pronounce him to be a bore. Southey's complexion is still healthy mahogany-brown, with a fleece of white hair, and eyes that seem running at full gallop. Leigh Hunt, 'man of genius in the shape of a Cockney,' is my near neighbor, full of quips and cranks, with good humor and no common sense. Old Rogers, with his pale head, white, bare and cold as snow, will work on you with those large blue eyes, cruel, sorrowful, and that sardonic shelf-chin. . . ." Who could resist such a branch of golden apples?

On a sunny afternoon in the following July, Emerson and Carlyle were strolling together at Stonehenge. The larks were singing overhead, and the wind was blowing the buttercups in the meadows. They clambered over the stones, counted and measured them, and talked of the flight of ages. Carlyle was in a gentle mood; he spoke of the old times of England, the acts of the saints, the men who built the cathedrals. Emerson and he had had their differences: they had found themselves worlds apart in their views of the nineteenth century, for more and more Carlyle had come to believe in the doctrines of work and force as ends in themselves. But this ancient sphinx of a temple put all these petty dissensions out of sight.

For nine months Emerson had been traveling in England, lecturing in Manchester, London, Edinburgh, Glasgow, observing, going to school. His journals were packed with notes, enough to make a book of English Traits; he had dropped his net into this teeming sea and drawn up what a draught of fishes! Carlyle still seemed the largest man in England, but he had basked in half the glories of the country. He had even seen Wordsworth again at Rydal Mount, very old now and sleeping on his sofa, but soon roused when the talk turned to the new French Revolution. (He was bitter against the French, bitter against Carlyle—"a pest to the English tongue," but a fine healthy old man, with his corrugated face; and Emerson still thought that, with all the torpid places in his mind, the something hard and sterile in his poetry, the want of grace and variety, Wordsworth alone in his time had treated the human soul with an absolute trust.)

With Carlyle his relations had been somewhat disappointing. "Well, here we are, shoveled together again!" Carlyle had said, standing in the door with a lamp, when Emerson arrived at ten o'clock at night. They had met with much affection and talked far and wide before going to bed, but in the morning Carlyle had changed. "What has brought you over to the old country?" he said. "Surely not to 'lecture.' Aren't there enough windbags in Lancashire?" He thought Emerson was a fool to waste his time palavering to Paisley weavers and mechanics; he had grown very cynical and sour; he bespattered the whole world with his oil of vitriol. They found they had little in common; but for Emerson his friend was still the bravest scholar in England, and he was glad to listen. Carlyle was all for murder, money and punishment by death, for slavery and every petty abomination. You praised republics, and he liked the Czar of Russia; you admired free trade and found him a Protectionist; you upheld the freedom of the press, and he wished nothing so much as to turn all the reporters out of Parliament; you stood for free institutions, he for a stringent government that showed people what to do and made them do it. But in all this he plainly revered realities; he anathematized decorum and respectability; he worshiped fortitude and enthusiasm. And, as Emerson said to himself, he had carried his life erect, made himself a power confessed by all men, taught scholars their lofty duty and scornfully taught the nobles. A hammer that crushed mediocrity and pretension. A divining rod for all that was real and sound.

Macaulay was another story. In his talk what fire, speed, fury, talent and effrontery! The king of diners-out, but with no affirma-

tive quality, Emerson thought: a historian whose sole interest was
to glorify every sort of material advantage. (What a notable green-
grocer was spoiled to make Macaulay!) But he had liked George
Stephenson, the inventor of the locomotive: the man who created
a material good brought something into the world—a very different thing from the philosopher who said that such goods as these
were the ends of life. He had liked Tennyson too, when they dined
together at the house of Coventry Patmore. For this musky poet
of gardens and parks and palaces, so rich in fancy, so powerful in
language, with a coloring like Titian, color like the dawn, for
"Ulysses" and "Oenone" he had long been thankful: a perfect
music box, Tennyson, for all manner of delicate tones and rhythms.
And there he was at Patmore's, with his quiet, sluggish strength, a
talking Hawthorne, Carlyle's "best man in England to smoke a
pipe with." And in Edinburgh he had seen De Quincey, a gentle
little elf, with an old, old face, shabbily dressed, with exquisite
speech and manners, who had walked in from the country ten
miles on the muddy roads and had *not* spoken like the organ of
York Minster. He was quite serene and happy, like a child of
seven, telling how he had been robbed by two girls in the street,
talking of Landor's *Hellenics* and of *Paradise Regained,* and how
he had lost five manuscript books of Wordsworth's unpublished
poems. A few days later, Emedson dined with him at Lasswade,
where he lived with his three daughters, and De Quincey came
back in the coach to hear Emerson lecture. As they entered Edinburgh, De Quincey grew very nervous, until one of the company
assured him that his old enemy, the landlady Mrs. MacBold, had
moved to another quarter of the town.

Emerson had made up his mind to miss nothing interesting or
significant. Never in all his life had he dreamed of so many dinners,
breakfasts, receptions (where he found himself the "parlour Ere-
bus" of old). He had gone to breakfast, of course, at Samuel

Rogers', that museum of art and anecdote; talked with Disraeli, Prince Albert, Lord Palmerston, Rothschild; spent an evening with Dickens in John Forster's rooms; visited Turner's studio, and Kew Gardens with Hooker; and Robert Owen had taken him through the Hunterian Museum. And how many other personages he had met, each of whom contributed to his gallery of human nature!— Leigh Hunt, Thackeray, Milman, the Duchess of Sutherland, Faraday, Mrs. Jameson. A young fellow of Oriel, Arthur Hugh Clough, fascinated by his lectures, had invited him to Oxford; and there he had talked with some of the younger writers, Froude and Matthew Arnold. Clough and Arnold had been much bewildered by Carlyle, and Arnold had written a sonnet in honor of Emerson's *Essays.*

He had gone to Paris for a month. Clough had come over too, and they had dined together daily at a *table d'hôte.* The Revolution of May had broken out, and the streets were full of soldiers; and one day, looking out of his window, Emerson had seen a crowd of furious horses dragging cannon towards the National Assembly. He had spent an evening at Barbès' *Club de la Revolution,* and another at Citizen Blanqui's Club, where the workmen in their blouses spoke with a fire and a deep sincerity that were good to hear; and on May 15 it looked as if the Revolution were going to succeed. But Blanqui and Barbès, who had reigned for a quarter of an hour, were fast in jail by night. Emerson had not really known the French before, and he found himself rapidly correcting his preconceptions. He heard Lamartine speak on the Polish question and Michelet lecture on philosophy. He saw Rachel in *Phèdre* and two other plays and was struck by the terror, the demoniacal power she threw into passages of defiance and denunciation, by the raging fire within her, by the intellectual cast of her manners and carriage. The gaiety and politeness of the people, the fountains and parks and gardens were an endless pleasure; and he said to himself that, if hard should come to hard, and he needed some refuge of solitude and independence, he would always remember Paris.

More lectures in London followed. A letter had appeared in one of the papers urging him to speak at a price sufficiently low to allow poor literary men to hear him; for "Emerson," the writer said, "is a phenomenon whose like is not in the world, and to miss him is to lose an important part out of the Nineteenth Century." So he read three lectures in Exeter Hall, on "Domestic Life," "Shakespeare" and "Napoleon"; and now he had lingered on till July, with what a store of impressions! This island, stuffed full in every corner and crevice, with towns, towers, churches, villas, palaces; the number and power of the trades and guilds, the military strength and splendor, the multitudes of remarkable men and women; the old men, red as roses, with their clear skins and peach-bloom complexions; the vigor and brawn of the people (castles compared with Americans), their sound animal structure, their freedom and personal courage had filled him with an ever-increasing respect. A sensible, handsome, powerful race, a population of lords, he was ready to call them. The best of actual nations.

What manners, too, what talent turned into manners! He had caught many a glimpse, perceived many a trait, of that Aristocracy, that dim superior race, unrealized as yet in humanity, of which he had always dreamed. But that race was a race of gods, not lords, commensurate with Nature, all-comprehending, disdainful of the world. The English stood in awe of mundane facts; they confined their aspirations to the means of dealing with facts, and they valued only the faculties that enabled them to do so. In America, he felt, as he turned his face towards home—but he couldn't clearly express the feeling that filled him. Thin and pale the New World danced before bloodshot English eyes. But the New World was a faith, and he lived in the light of it.

✪

Mr. Emerson in the Lecture Room

Boston, April 28, 1870

Dear ———:

I have the happiness of being one of thirty persons who attend a course of lectures by Mr. Emerson, intended for the graduates of Harvard. . . . His general topic is "Notes on the History of the Intellect," and he began his first lecture with a witty disclaimer against being considered a metaphysician himself, in any ordinary acceptation of that term. He said that Reid, Hamilton, Berkeley, Kant, give us less, with all their systems, than Montaigne, Montesquieu, Diderot, or even Rabelais, with his breadth of humor.

The piece that follows is a long one. It is apt to seem even longer to today's reader. Its organization is chancy, its content often nebulous, its tone old-fashioned. Yet in a way it is the pivotal piece in this book. The aim of this Profile is to show us something of the character of a noted man. If the noted man is an author, it is impossible to separate his character entirely from his writing; no knife can cut the two. But it is certainly possible to emphasize one instead of the other and that has been attempted here.

A problem remains, however. It is to get a sense of the author's work in relation to his character and, specifically, to find a piece that will provide that sense for us. In Emerson's case, it is surprisingly difficult. F. O. Matthiessen has done a brilliant study of Emerson's mind and art as part of our American renaissance. Sherman Paul and Stephen Whicher have produced books on Emerson the writer that have in common an admirable insight and an ordering of Emerson's mind. On what may be a questionable

"The trouble is," he continued, "men ordinarily take no note of
their thoughts. They say one thing today and another thing tomorrow, and forget them all. Our thoughts are our companions and
our guides; but sometimes we find ourselves less familiar with
these interior friends than with exterior ones. It is the development
of mind which makes the science of mind.

"The miracle is the tally of thoughts to things. A new thought
is retrospective. It is like fire applied to a train of gunpowder. It
lights all that has gone before.

"We are impatient of too much introspection. What the eye sees,
and not the eye, is what we chiefly regard. We are broken into
sparkles of thought, like the stars in the system of Copernicus. To

---

premise, I have decided not to draw from any of them. I have turned from
those critics because they were too penetrating, too coherent for my purpose: they gave *their* order to Emerson. What I wanted was the feel of
Emerson's writing. I wanted to give the reader the impression that James
Russell Lowell, for one, received and then put into his satirical verses. He
is talking about Emerson's poetry but his words apply equally to Emerson's
prose: "In the worst of his poems are mines of rich matter,/But thrown in
a heap with a crush and a clatter." I wanted to give the impression of a
miscellaneous mixture of idealism, exhortation, and example.

Because I found nothing in today's books or articles on Emerson which
gave me precisely that, I turned to those of yesterday, I found what I
wanted in an essay from the 1880's by Annie Fields. It showed Emerson in
the process of testing his writing; it showed him on the lecture platform
reading what would become his essays. Her article is couched in the form
of a long, rambling letter to a friend. It contains the gist of a course of
lectures as she remembered it. At times the letter is tedious, just as Emerson was at times tedious. But it reveals something of the wisdom and inspiration of Emerson, something even of the mystery of his pronouncements. And it seems to me to give a true feeling for Emerson.

The article, then, is made up mostly of quotations, as recalled imperfectly by a devoted listener. Yet it is essential Emerson, offering us a view
of his character we would not otherwise have.

Annie Fields was an author in her own right in addition to being the
wife of the Boston publisher, James T. Fields. She wrote poetry and essays
and also acted as the mistress of a highly literary *salon*. Her "Mr. Emerson
in the Lecture Room," here abridged, appeared in the *Atlantic Monthly*,
LI (June 1883), 818–832.

Be is the great mystery! We are angles; each one makes an angle with Truth. Our thoughts are like facets cut on the jewel of Truth. Intellect is not a gift, but the presence of God."

You will see from these morsels that I attempt nothing like a report in your behalf. Few things disturb Mr. Emerson so much as to see a notebook; so we only have a right to carry away what we can put into the pocket of our memories. He seldom speaks an hour; once he gave us but twenty minutes; indeed, I think half an hour is about the measure of his discourse. He said one day, "The mind is what has and sees and is seen. There is perfect unison between mind and matter; hence the value of a new word, which is a gift to the world. Plato gave us one of the most valuable words and definitions when he used 'analogy,' and defined it as 'identity of ratios.' No definition of 'genius,' however, can equal the word, and Mr. Carlyle's book on Heroism is at once outdone to the gentle mind by the presence of the hero.

"The best study of metaphysics is physics. The subtle relations between things, the discovery that every system is but a part of the one great system—this is the wonderful lesson the universe teaches us.

"There is no stop; all is pulsation, undulation. The world is framed of atoms, and in every atom we may discern Man.

"Growth and birth and the sexes—all these words belong also to the mind; for there is assuredly sex in the mind, though not the same. A masculine mind is sometimes found in the woman, and a feminine in the man.

"The mind is a deep, unfathomable cavern. Man is forever a stranger to himself, and what a blessing is he who can help us to a better acquaintance! What a torch is that which can throw one gleam down into the spirit's cavernous depths! We are to each other as our perception is. Perception is power. The first apprehension is the germ from which all science results.

"Thoughts are rare; whoever has one to give, that person is

needed. Young people often feel as if they were bursting with them; but when they try to deliver themselves, it is discovered to be all a false alarm. The heavens appear to be sown with countless stars; but when we try to number those we really see, they only amount to a few hundreds. So it is with our thoughts. Herschel computed there were only about one hundred hours in the year when his great forty-foot telescope was of any avail for observations. Our hours of thought are as rare. It is not every undisturbed day which is fruitful in them. They belong to happy periods.

"Perception is swiftness; they who see first what to do can do it first, except some few inspired idiots, who are full and see much, but cannot be tapped anywhere. Words and definitions are often the result of this swift apprehension. Perception helps expression, which is but partial at best. If we could once but free our thought, we should be liberated into the universe.

"Talent is ever in demand. A man who can do anything well is needed. We utilize talent too much in this age. It goes for nothing if it be not lucrative. A useful talent is wanted twelve hours in the day.

"Bohemianism is the surrender of talent to money. Isocrates said of Protagoras, and that class of philosophers, that they would sell anything but their hope in the immortality of their own souls for four minae. Talent is everywhere in great repute with us. To say clever things, to be sharp and brilliant, is to be well regarded."

Mr. Emerson seldom announces any subject or subdivision of his general topic, but one afternoon he began by saying, "My subject is 'Memory.' Every machine must be perfect to be in running order. Wheels, cogs, teeth, must all match and hold well together. It is the healthy mind whose memory works perfectly. Memory should shut tight on its subject as the jaws of a bulldog. It is cement, bitumen, matrix, to the mind, the cohesion which creates knowledge. It is retroactive, working backward as well as forward in an ever-lengthening chain. Akin to the power of creation is the joy of calling back into existence, by the compelling force of will, something which had disappeared from life.

"Tenacity, accessibility or choice, and swiftness are qualities of memory. No memory holds a variety of subjects. We remember according to our affections. Napoleon could remember the army roll, but said his memory was so poor that an Alexandrine verse was impossible to him. If the army roll were put on one side, and all the great poems of the world on the other, he should choose the army roll. He wrote down everything else which it was important to record; *that* he remembered without an effort.

"Quintilian has. said, 'Memory is the measure of mind.' Frederick the Great knew every man in his army and every bottle in his wine cellar. Boileau, coming to read a poem to Daguesseau, many pages in length, the latter, on Boileau's ceasing to read, immediately repeated the whole after him, saying he had heard it before. Boileau was at first distressed, but soon discovered it to be simply a feat of memory. Dr. Johnson could repeat whole books which he had read but once. This power failed somewhat after he was forty years old.

"The faculty of memory does not appear to grow; there is some wildness in it. Horses possess in their wild state a swiftness which is never attained after they are broken; so the sleep of savages and children, which people of culture and care never know again. Such is the undisturbed power of memory in childhood. We never forget what is absorbed in those few first years of existence. The power of vivid remembrance seems to make time very long to children. We hear one who can scarcely speak say to his companion, 'Can't you remember how we used to make mud pies and play in puddles?'— yet perhaps it was to us a very short time before, though seeming years to them. This wild memory belongs both to children and to the childhood of the world. There is an Eastern poem in existence, said to be longer than the *Iliad* and *Odyssey,* which exists only in the memories of its people.

"Memory is not only subject to will, but it has a will of its own. It is like a looking glass, because it reflects what passes before it; yet, unlike a looking glass, it retains, and at will reproduces, any figure that is wanted in the very center of the plate. What the power is by which a subject is often unconsciously retained, through years, uncalled for, and is suddenly produced when needed, no one has ever been able to turn himself inside out quick enough to discover.

"There is a bit of journal, written by an English gentleman after a pleasant visit to a country house, in which he says, 'I left Lady ———'s house several days ago. I heard many good things there which I have been intending to set down, but have not yet found time. I take a look at them now and then, in my memory, to be sure they are quite safe.'

"Who of us has not known kindred experiences! Memory accelerates life, and lengthens it. How a short period may be made a long one by a diversity of subjects being presented to us which are worth remembering, we all know. So a person of quick perception to behold and memory to secure will be possessed of something of which a slower man, having the same experience, may be altogether unconscious of. What a convenience and resource is memory! To have what is needed always on demand! It was said of a German professor that he was a third university; he carried a whole library in his head.

"This memory is after all so rare that let a man read what everybody else has read, just one year later and he will appear to other people to be a sphinx. The swiftness of memory distinguishes it. To immediately produce the thing wanted—that is the point. It is no marvel to see anybody perform the feats of Safford with pen and paper. Everybody can do that! But at the age of ten, with a multiplicand of fifteen figures and a multiplier of fifteen figures, to give the result at once, was indeed a marvel, and this ten years before he came to our university. Nevertheless, memory appears to be no test of the original power of the mind. With a certain ideal class it seems rather to interfere. Wordsworth and Goethe, for instance, could never bring the memory to explain the meaning and connection of certain passages written in their youth. Whatever coherence there was in their own minds with what went before or came after was not easily perceived by others, nor to be explained by themselves. Not unfrequently, however, the connection between thoughts, lost by the author, may be discovered by other imaginative minds brought to bear upon the subject. There is something ideal in memory. What is addressed to the imagination is oftentimes retained, if everything beside be lost. When we discover that a man remembers many things we have not; when we perceive that he does not do this by a knot in his handkerchief, or a bit of worsted, or by any trick, but by some hidden and fine relation between subject and subject, which we cannot discern, then we feel the greatness of the power, and we seem to talk with Jove.

"The memory of beautiful things retards time; music conceals it. Thus the allegory of Siva, when he comes to ask the god to give him one of three princes in marriage for his daughter. As he approaches the oracle he hears sounds of music, which appear to him so beautiful that he delays awhile to listen; and while he delays the first strain ceases, and another begins, which he also waits to hear. When at last there is silence he asks the god for one of the three princes. He is assured that it is impossible; for not only the three princes, but all their children and great-grand-children to the third generation, have already married while he was listening to the music.

"Memory, with most people, consists of a record of what notes are given and when the payment is due; with others, it is formative and a token of love. We naturally hate all docked or shallow-thoughted men. Simonides is called the Father of Memory. It is recorded on the tomb of Abelard that he knew all that was knowable. The best office of memory is to forget all that is painful, and

remember only our joys. Fate is an artist, and lets us forget what
we should forget. Most of us remember only what we have remembered before; but deep thought holds in solution all facts. The
best art of memory is to understand things thoroughly. New
knowledge always calls upon old knowledge. Memory should
enshrine principles instead of traditions."

The serious significance of this lecture was lightened for the
public mind by a number of humorous illustrations. Mr. Emerson
said that there were various directions as to how memory may
be acquired. "I remember reading," he continued, "in an old
book called Fullom's *Casket of Memory,* that it is good to make
a gargle, to be taken warm in the morning, to be composed of
a concoction of flowers, new milk, and pennyroyal! Dr. Johnson
said he could remember the man he had kicked last." Speaking,
one day, of imagination, Mr. Emerson quoted Sir Thomas Browne,
who said, "The severe schools shall never laugh me out of the
philosophy of Hermes, that this visible world is but a picture of
the invisible, wherein as in a portrait, things are not, truly, but in
equivocal shapes, and as they counterfeit some more real substance
in that invisible fabric."

"No one, perhaps, has given us a better exposition of this doctrine than Emmanuel Swedenborg. The substance of his teaching is
how, out of the shows of things, to obtain reality. Imagination
predicts Nature, and leads our thought upward from point to point.
To discern the thought beneath the form is its office. The imagination following the steps of a new thought hears it echoed from
pole to pole. The symbol plays a large part in our speech. We
could not do without it. Few can either give or receive unrelieved
thought in conversation. A symbol or trope lightens it. We remember a happy comparison all our lives. Machiavelli said the papacy
was a great stone in the wound of Italy to keep it from healing.
Genius shows itself in sprightly suggestion. A good analogy to my
thought is far more to me than to find that Plato or Swedenborg

agree with it. To find that the elm tree nods assent to it and that running waters conform to it—this alone is confirmation.

"Dante's poetry has hands and feet. I went into a painter's studio once, where I found he had modeled the figures of Dante's characters in clay before beginning to paint his picture; and I was half persuaded the poet did the same himself."

All this seems like a wretched prose translation of what Mr. Emerson said. The lectures themselves are poetry and music. Speaking of dreams, he continued, "More than what Plato or any philosopher can or ever shall give us is sometimes unveiled in these unaccountable experiences. No drama in five acts ever written can compare with the drama in fifty acts unfolded to the dirtiest sluggard upon the floor of the watch-house.

"The words 'Fancy' and 'Imagination' are frequently used without discrimination. It is a mistake. Fancy is full of accidental surprises, and amuses the vacant or idle mind. Imagination silences Fancy, which becomes speechless in its presence. Imagination deals with the identity of things. It is real, central, tragic. Sometimes we think it makes all we call 'Nature.'

"My friend Thoreau was full of fanciful suggestions from natural objects: such as 'the tanager setting the woods on fire as he flies through them'; 'the goldenrod waving its yellow banners, and marching eastward to the Crusade'; 'the dewy cobwebs, handkerchiefs dropped by fairies.' And of Wachusett as seen from Concord he used to say, 'Look at the back of that great whale just under our bows! They have stuck a harpoon in him, and he is plowing his way off across the continent.' I can never see it without that thought coming again to my mind. Imagination gives us the like romantic elements for our life, and feeds us with commanding thoughts.

"Everyone would be a poet if his intellectual digestion were perfect.

"The transition from the subject of 'Imagination' to that of 'Inspiration' is easy. No fable of metamorphosis, but a truth, is this which inspiration works in us. Plato has said no man who always understands himself can ever be a poet. There is an essence which passes from an intelligence higher than ourselves, and sways us. We cannot compel it by our will. We throw up our work for it (wishing it may come), to no purpose. When we least hope for it in lyric glances, it shines upon us. Unstable in its course, it fills the agitated soul.

"Wordsworth said he cared little for those poets who understood what they did, like Byron and Scott. He much preferred William Blake. We never know the depth of the notes we accidentally sound. Heat is necessary. We must have heat. Enthusiasm daring ruin for its object.

"Pit-coal—where to find it! We may have engines which work as perfectly as watches, but they are all nothing if we cannot strike the mine.

"There is contagion in inspiration. It was said of Mirabeau that 'tomorrow was no impostor to him'; all who came near him learned how much the hours meant to him. We love to be magnetized.

"The story of Pleiades—by what poet has it not been sung! Every nun in retirement makes the lost Pleiad the subject of her song. I think there must be a universal chord struck in the idea, which is that of a lost thought. How to obtain thoughts is the question.

"Condensation, concentration, high flights of the soul—these are some of the means by which thoughts visit us. But there is no continuance, no permanency, in their presence. They are subject to continual ebb and flow; beside, we lose much by the breaking up of hours and by sleep. We are sometimes like the cat's back, breaking out all over in sparkles of thought. Are these moods within control? Where is the Franklin for this fluid? Poetry is full of apostrophe to inspiration, much of it commonplace enough; but Herrick's little poem is worth reading; also the preface written by William Blake to his poems. A certain recognition of this power beyond themselves is often manifested by great men, as when Kepler said he could afford to wait one hundred years for a reader, since God had waited five thousand years for such an astronomer as himself.

"How many sources of inspiration can we count? As many as are our affinities. First, I would say health; second, sleep. Life is in short periods; cut into strips, as it were. We lie down spent; we rise with powers new born. As a third source of inspiration I would choose solitary converse with nature. What student does not know this? The mornings, the deep woods, the yellow autumntime. There is much in that French motto, *'Il n'y a que le matin.'* Thought is clear then; life is new and strong. But to save the hours, to prevent the frightening away of thought! It is a difficult problem. At home I shut myself up, frequently with great detriment to my affairs (being small farmer as well as householder), and must not be interrupted. But the only safe refuge is a country inn or a city hotel. There no one can call you, and the hours flow on in astronomic leisure. Years ago, I remember, Mr. Carlyle projected a study at the top of his house, subject to no housemaid. Late in life this plan of his was accomplished, and Frederick the Great was the result. Cold is another enemy. George Sand says, somewhere, she never had an idea that the slightest chill could not drive away from her. To some, a fine view, the face of external nature, is a hindrance. William Blake said nature was a disturbance to his work. Sir Joshua Reynolds disliked Richmond, and said his landscape was the human face divine.

"We remember the plainness of Goethe's study. New poetry, too, is inspiration. I mean for the most part old poetry read for the first time; so also with new words. Almost we say, not even friends! a word is best.

"Next, I would put conversation. Good conversation is a wonderful promoter of intellectual activity. We become emulous. If one says better things than we could, or different, we are stimulated in turn. Conversation is the right metaphysical professor. Sincere and happy conversation always doubles our power."

On another day, in approaching the subject of "Genius," Mr. Emerson said, "Walter Scott described it as Perseverance, and it has also been described as Attention; but I hold that Genius is Veracity, and with it always the year is one and the emperor present. With Genius there is always youth, and never the obituary eloquence of memory. Who taught Raphael and Correggio to paint? They were taught of God in a dream.

"Shakespeare, Voltaire, Byron, Daniel Webster, and Father Taylor were equally interesting to all classes; for there are two brains in every man of genius. Talent is vice-president and presiding officer, never the king. Truth is sensibility to the laws of the world, and genius is always governed by truth. Genius deals with the elemental, the roots of things, and takes nothing second hand."

Once, in speaking of common sense, Mr. Emerson said, "It is a power all esteem. It reaps, plows, sows, threshes, sweats. No one would be without it. Bonar said, 'Common sense and genius make the world,' not wit; that is only a side issue. Artists affect sticking to facts. Goethe was full of this. Like Pericles, he needed a helmet to conceal the dreaded infirmity of his head. He had a large air-chamber; but if any of his neighbors caught him creeping into the chamber of the Muses, he would deny it point-blank, saying, 'No, no; I was going to the county jail.' Some nations appear more distinguished for this quality than others. I think the English excel; although with them it is apt to degenerate into brutality. The French people perhaps manage it more courteously; yet a republic is a better field for its development. With a monarchy and the small circle of aristocracy come idealism and exemption. In a republic all find use for hands and feet. Napoleon conversing with an officer on a matter of business, the functionary said, 'I can hardly talk with you as I should like about this, for I am not a

witty man.' Napoleon answered, 'I do not want your wit. I want
the work!' One of the German princes, to whom Mr. Osborne, of
England, was sent as minister, being interested in ghostly appearances, assured Mr. Osborne, if he would accompany him at twelve
o'clock midnight to the neighboring churchyard, he would show
him a ghost. 'If I may take six grenadiers with me, who shall
shoot at the apparition when it comes, I will accompany your
majesty gladly,' was the reply. The rendezvous did not take place.
The Duke of Wellington having a bulletproof shirt brought him by
the inventor, 'Bulletproof, you say?' asked the duke. 'Yes,' was the
reply. 'Will you put it on yourself, and allow me to order in six
soldiers to shoot at it?' The man did not press his suit—nor wear it.
Lord Palmerston, being asked to serve on the cholera committee
in Edinburgh, declined, saying, 'They would do better to obey the
laws of health.' Sir Fowell Buxton's book is full of common sense
regarding Parliament and the character of speeches there. Many
of the rules he lays down would be good for more Parliaments than
that of England.

"Common sense was a great characteristic of Dr. Johnson, and
his conversation can never be overrated. It will live when much
of the Rambler will be forgotten.

"The primal facts of Intellect lie close under the surface of
Nature. Sometimes we feel Nature to be a chamber lined with
mirrors, wherein we see reflected the disguised man. The analogy
between processes of thought and those of the physical world is
perfect, thorough. Good work does itself; there is growth in the
night.

"The fame of the Mons pear came from the saliency of the trees
as well as the excellence of the fruit. The shoots were continually
cut off and new graftings made. Saliency of the mind may be encouraged by use. We need saliency. Nothing is more simple than
the fact discovered yesterday, nothing more wonderful than the
fact to be discovered tomorrow. In the old schools of Italy they

would dry up a man to make a grammarian. We will hope that the mended humanity of republics will save us.

"We are inspired by every kind of true vigor. We do not need to meet vigor of our own kind, but misalliance, misassociation, must be shunned. It is of no avail. Genius ill-companioned is no genius; without identity of base, chaos must be forever. We are surprised by occult sympathies. In each form of nature we seem to see ourselves in some distorting glass. Nature is saturated with Deity. The solar architecture, upon which we gaze in wonder, is not so marvelous as the same system in the revolving mind.

"Thoughts run parallel with the creative law; to unveil them, to understand their action from the laws of the world—this is imagination, this is the poetic gift. Among the laws of the mind are powers and analogies which should be considered. First among them stands Identity; then follow Metamorphosis, Flux" . . . Here Mr. Emerson paused, his sentence still unfinished, while he seemed to search among his papers for its conclusion. After a few moments, finding nothing to advance the subject satisfactorily, he rose, and so ended the lecture of the day.

On another occasion Mr. Emerson renewed this subject. "The detachment and flux of our natures," he said, "are the meters of their strength. Nothing remains; everything is becoming other than it is; this doctrine is the secret of things. Wisdom consists in keeping the soul fluent, resisting petrifaction. We see this in all things; we are asked why there is a hole in the bottom of the flowerpot! The moment there is fixation, petrifaction and death ensue. The very word "Nature" makes us to know this: *'natura'; becoming about to be born*. We are immortal by the force of transits. The law of the world is transition, and our power lies in that. No wonder children delight in masks and plays—in being other than they are; so do older children; it is the instinct of the universe.

"Pace is yet another power or quality of mind. The swift mind is capable of spiritual sculpture, and can build a statue in the air with every word. The artist values himself on his speed. Saadi says, 'With the budding out of the leaf this work began, and was ended with the falling of the same.' Shakespeare seems to have lived faster than any other man; he appears to have been a thousand years old when he wrote his first line, and his judgment is as wonderful to us as his pace. Quick wit is always a miracle, but for *l'esprit de l'escalier* we have no respect; everybody has that. Good fortune is only another name for quick perceptions. Improvisation is simply acceleration. We have nothing of value in literature done that way; what is gained in one direction is lost in another. It is thought our pace is injured by civilization; untutored peoples are said to do what they do more rapidly than we. When results are shown to us without the processes by which they were produced, we are lost in wonder. In this way Sir George Beaumont made Wilkie's sudden reputation in London. He went about saying, 'Here's a young man who has just come to London, who went at once to see a picture by Teniers, and then ran home and painted "The Village Politicians."'

"Each power, when largely developed, exhausts some other. The Delphian prophetess at her altar is herself a victim. But the pace of Nature is strong! We never hear that she has sprained her foot. We become spent, and fail; she thanks 'God that she breathes very well.'

"We find grown people, with quick perceptions, whose judgment is two years old—Hercules with a withered arm! This element of Time is a wonderful magician. I once went to a beautiful *fête*, where was a little old man in a gray coat. Presently some one asked him for one of Dolland's great telescopes; and he produced it immediately, no larger at first than a microscope, from his waistcoat pocket. Soon after a lady stepped up, and said she should like a Turkey carpet laid on the lawn, if he had one about him; and the little gray man took that out, too, and presently a marquee was added to the rest. Time, the little gray man, has made, and is making, changes as wonderful upon every one of us. No Turkey carpets nor marquee tents can be so extraordinary as the processes in chemistry, miraculous to our uninstructed eyes.

"Bias is yet another quality or power of the mind to be considered—power to resist shocks of contending temperaments. Faraday discovered that certain minerals would obey the two poles of the magnet, north and south, while others would only seek those diametrically opposed. Polarity is a universal law; every mind is a magnet, with a new north.

"We soon discern whether a man speaks from himself, or is giving us something at second hand. We see through all his paint; he may as well wash it off at once. He who made the world lets that speak for itself, and does not employ a town crier. So shall each soul speak for itself as God made it. Opinions are organic. They should be fostered by our studies into a healthy natural growth. We say of a man, 'Where is his home?' There where he is incessantly called.

"Do not fear to push these individualizations to their farthest divergence. Excellence is an inflamed personality. Power fraternizes with power, and wishes you to be not like himself. We acquiesce in what we are. We do not wish conformity or fair words; yea and nay will suffice. God makes but one man of each kind. 'My son will not be like me, and can never fill my place,' said Napoleon, 'but he will fulfill his own destiny.' A human soul is a momentary fixation of power. The tenacity of retention must be in proportion to the idea it represents.

"Everybody can do his best work easiest. While the master works in his own way, and draws on his own power, he cannot be supplanted. Man resents the rule which cripples him. We must do our best in our own way. We do not wish praise; we never forgive overappreciation. Reserve, pique—both these can help to stimulate us. Do not fear to be a monotone! We wish every man to truly please himself; then he will please us."

Mr. Emerson read in connection with this subject a passage from Varnhagen von Ense upon vicarious sacrifice. He said it was so fine that it would not be out of place anywhere, and belonged to the philosophy of history.

One day he remarked that he had always considered a course of lectures at Harvard University would be incomplete if a series upon Plato and the Platonists were omitted. "Thought has subsisted for the most part on one root; the Norse mythology, the Vedas, Shakespeare, have served for ages. The history of our venerable Bible—what heights, what lights, what strength, does this contain! We see how Nature loves to cross her stocks; the invaded by the invader. We see this in the history of the Aryans, of the Pelasgi as invaded by the Ionians, of the East by Alexander, and so on continually. There must be both power and provocation to develop the highest in man.

"The systems of philosophy are few, and repeat each other; there is little that is new. One philosopher unfolds the doctrine of materialism; the next will unfold the same doctrine, but after the fashion of his own mind; another will dispute sense and talk non-sense; the fourth will take a middle ground, until we have Materialism, Idealism, Dogmatism, Skepticism, and few new thoughts.

"When Orientalism in Alexandria found the Platonists, a new school was produced. The sternness of the Greek school, feeling its way forward from argument to argument, met and combined with the beauty of Orientalism. Plotinus, Proclus, Porphyry, and Jamblicus were the apostles of the new philosophy.

"Some truths were then, perhaps, first unveiled: such as, pure power is more felt than anything purely intellectual; Mind is the source of things, the truth of absolute units; Being, or First Cause, creates to the end of imparting happiness. This philosophy was the consolation of the human race. The principles of Plato were distilled in various schools, and at last went down with the greatness of Rome. Then came, not until the third century of our era, Plotinus. He was the founder of the new Platonism. The wisdom of its method is great and worthy of profound study. Music, Love, Philosophy, were the three powers of which he has left us a beautiful analysis." Mr. Emerson read carefully selected passages from Plotinus, and afterward gave the history of his life so far as it is known; then, taking up an octavo volume translated by Thomas Taylor, of Norwich, which contained the essay of Synesius on "Providence," he spoke of its untold value to the world. His audience could understand at least how precious the book was to him. Doubtless many a reader, remembering his words concerning it, has turned its mystic pages; but the readers must be few who have seen the mysterious light shining in them which the poet found.

Of Proclus Mr. Emerson said, "I am always astonished at his strength. He has purple deeps which I can never fully sound. What literature should be, he is. Proclus first called attention to Chaldaic oracles. There are hardly men athletic enough to read him. How insignificant and far behind Proclus is what we call Scotch philosophy. It is like comparing Phidias and Uncle Toby.

"For a period of the world's history Plato and the Platonists were almost lost, as it appeared. But the disciples always reappear; thus, curiously, in our age have these doctrines revived. As surely as Wilkinson is the pupil of Swedenborg, and as surely as everything must come round, so here in our time arrives a scholar who sets the Platonists on their legs again, and calls everybody to hear these sages who wrote fifteen hundred years ago. Thomas Taylor was a man of singular character: a rugged Englishman, without one refreshing stroke of wit, or even of good sense, haughtily believing in his work, he accepted poverty proudly to the end of its accomplishment. He cannot suppress his high contempt for those who are ignorant of Greek philosophy. He equals Gibbon in his pride, and Johnson in his gloom. There is little recorded of his life, but I draw much of my information from Porson. Thomas Taylor says, 'No living author beside myself has devoted himself to Plato.' Elsewhere he speaks of his 'solitary road'; and indeed it was a road no man had traversed for centuries. Niebuhr has a touching reference to him; the name is not given, but it can be no one else. Sydenham also, whom I should hardly quote here but for his strange fate and the interest his early death excites in us.

"Taylor tilts against many notable windmills. Like Coleridge, he thanked God that he knew no French. He calls Christianity a gigantic impiety. Like Winckelmann, he was a man born out of due time. Taylor had no faith in the education of the masses; his whole idea of government was founded on Plato's republic; he eagerly dissuaded the uneducated from reading his books. He received scorn for scorn. Even learned England knew nothing of him, gave him no attention. Hallam had never heard of him, nor Milman, nor, I think, had Macaulay. I met a gentleman who thought he could find out something for me, but the whole result of the inquiry was that Taylor's eldest son was named Proclus. There are very few facts beside. His wife married him suddenly, when she was about to be compelled to marry a rich man in his stead, and for a year or more they subsisted on seven shillings a week, which he made by copying. His labors were immense. Aristotle, Plato, Plotinus, Proclus, Synesius, all exist from his hand, and many other works. He was turned out of a good boarding-place because he wished to sacrifice a bull to Jupiter Olympus in the best parlor. His translation of Synesius will live with Comus, Laodamia, and a few other things of that nature."

The next afternoon Mr. Emerson said his subject was "The Conduct of the Intellect." "I have arranged," he continued, "with some amplitude the study of the working agents of the mind, that we may become conscious as far as possible how system and power may be reached by persons desirous of true culture. First, we will consider Attention, which is the natural prayer we make to Truth that she will discover herself to us. Attention is perpetual application of the will. Sir Isaac Newton said that what he had accomplished was done by always intending his mind. Goethe said that he believed every child should learn drawing; for it unfolds attention, the highest of our skills and virtues. This power cannot always be called into its fullest force, and it is differently excited in different persons, or in the same persons at different times. When you cannot flog your mind into power in your library, you go to family and friends, where it becomes refreshed. Some men have found the public their school and study. They go to their audience as others go to their closet, and learn there what they should say.

"This brings me again to Bias, that indispensable condition of all true influence. Each makes and should make one reserve in the canon of nature, namely, himself! Not the fact, but what he makes of it, is its value, after all. Be yourself! Don't walk one way and look another. Straining, *tour de force,* will accomplish for the time, but the result is always weariness and waste. You cannot disguise your opinions. This faculty is your lot in life; therefore make the most of it, instead of wishing it something else. Abandon yourself to your real love and hate! That which burns you can alone set other minds in flame. Labor, drudge, and wrestle for it; profound sincerity is the only basis of character. Beware of the temptation to patronize Providence. Set down a wise man in the center of a town, and he will create a new consciousness of wealth. He will show the rich their mistakes and poverty, and to the poor he will discover their own resources. He will establish an immovable equality.

"Most books of travel tell us nothing; but take the men born to travel and to see, and we recognize at once that they are inspired for discoverers. The poet sees also, and if he sees only in fragments he paints those with what energy he has.

"The primary quality of Genius is Veracity. 'What he would write, he was before he writ,' said Lord Brooke. Youth and truth

should be inseparable. No proselytizing adviser is then needed.
I want nothing less than Truth. I will wear her garment, rather
than array myself in a red rag of any borrowed garniture. I see how
grand it is.

"The condition of sanity is to keep down talent and to preserve
instinct. Otherwise we find talent substituted for genius, sensuality
for art. There is an organic order in every mind, therefore there
is natural order in our thought; but bad artists do not foresee
the end from the beginning."

Mr. Emerson here spoke of the Classic and Romantic schools of
art, and of the essential quality of Affirmation.

"The affirmative position of the mind," he continued; "knowing what we like best, and acknowledging it; discovering the grand
basis where lies the joy of the great masters that they are all alike;
not dealing with petty differences; not seeing less than the immortal—this is the duty of every healthy soul. It is the causal fact
in every forward nature that he shall look affirmatively upon subjects. An affirmative talker is always safe. I think it is the main
guard not to accept degrading views. Don't try to make the universe a blind alley. We must march under the banner of the ad-
vancing cause. There is no limit to the strength of affirmation; we
can go on, sky over sky and through soundless deeps, and the
follower learns that truth has steeps unapproachable to the pro-
fane foot. No negative evidence can be worth one affirmative. It is
the mind, never the body, which will conquer, and will burst up to
carry all away as with a sea-stroke. The true poet, if such could be
embodied, would electrify us with truth, once heard. What is now
the capital would be so no longer: grass would grow in its streets;
it would soon be superseded. Good order, analogy, health, benefit
—to each and all of these the assenting soul sings paean! Said a
good saint once to me, 'The Lord gives, but he never takes away.'
We must cleave to God against the name of God.

"I think Keats's best lines are those in 'Hyperion':

> So Saturn, as he walked into the midst,
> Felt faint, and would have sunk among the rest
> But that he met Enceladus's eye,
> Whose mightiness and awe of him at once
> Came like an inspiration.

"The contagion of an affirmative disposition is very great, and the gift or acquirement of this generosity is one of the consolations of life. Therefore use the faculty; labor, drudge, for it. Put to it the spirit of Napoleon when he was asked to repeat an order, and replied, 'Pensez, fripon! I never repeat; it is for you to remember.' Go, and be like Napoleon! Let his endeavor be your constant type and exemplar. He was always on the offensive, and, as he said himself, never on the defensive, except in the night, when he could not see his enemy. Use your powers, and put them to a better use than Napoleon put his. Use them all; otherwise we shall be like the Indians, with thick legs and thin arms. We need all our resources to live in the world which is to be used and decorated by us. Socrates understood this well. His humility was sincere, but he used it also with exquisite tact, making of it a better eyeglass to penetrate farther than the vision of other men.

"We must lie in wait for thoughts, for times when the intellect is facile; think with the flower of the soul. Be confident that a man cannot exhaust the abilities of his nature, and the best is never attained but at the price of continual labor. Success depends on previous preparation. If principles and high conduct be sustained by continual practice, their virtue will be inexhaustible. The question always is how to keep up to the top of my condition! . . ."

✪

Glimpses of Emerson

The perfect consistency of a truly great life, where inconsistencies of speech appear at once harmonized by the beauty of the whole, gives even to a slight incident the value of a bit of mosaic which, if omitted, would leave a gap in the picture. Therefore we never tire of "Whisperings" and "Talks" and "Walks" and "Letters" relating to the friends of our imagination, if not of our fireside, and insofar as such fragments bring men and women of achievement nearer to our daily lives, without degrading them, they warm and cheer us with something of their own beloved and human presences.

This feeling explains the publication of so many of these side-lights on the lives of what Emerson himself calls "superior people," and the following glimpses will only confirm what he expresses of such natures when he says, "In all the superior people I have met I notice directness, truth spoken more truly, as if

---

Immense though her admiration for Emerson was, Annie Fields never developed into an idolater. In this essay, occasioned like Whipple's by Emerson's death in 1882, she gathers together a miscellany of recollections about him. Her tone is uniformly kind but underneath there are honest and often interesting judgments. For example, she remarks on the fact that Emerson "could not easily forgive any one who made him laugh immoderately." The essay was published in *Harper's Magazine,* LXVIII (February 1884), 457–467.

everything of obstruction, of malformation, had been trained away."

In reading the correspondence between Carlyle and Emerson, few readers could fail to be impressed with the generosity shown by Emerson in giving his time and thought without stint to the publication of Carlyle's books in this country. Nor was this the single instance of his devotion to the advancement of his friends. In a brief memoir, lately printed, of Jones Very, as an introduction to a collection of his poems, we find a like record there.

After the death of Thoreau, Emerson spared no trouble to himself that his friend's papers might be properly presented to the reading world. He wrote to his publisher, Mr. Fields: "I send all the poems of Thoreau which I think ought to go with the letters. These are the best verses, and no other whole piece quite contents me. I think you must be content with a little book, since it is so good. I do not like to print either the prison piece or the John Brown with these clear sky-born letters and poems." After all his labor and his care, however, it was necessary to hold consultation with Thoreau's sister, and she could not find it in her heart to leave out some of the tender personalities which had grown more dear to her since her brother's death, and which had been omitted in the selection. She said that she was sure Mr. Emerson was not pleased at the restorations she made after his careful work of elimination was finished, but he was too courteous and kind to say much, or to insist on his own way; he only remarked, "You have spoiled my Greek statue." Neither was he himself altogether contented with his work, and shortly afterward said he would like to include "The Maiden in the East," "partly because it was written of Mrs. W———n, and partly because other persons like it so well."

"I looked over the poems again and again," he said, "and at last reserved but ten, finding some blemish in all the others which prevented them from seeming perfect to me. How grand is his poem about the mountains! As it is said of Goethe that he never spoke of the stars but with respect, so we may say of Thoreau and the mountains." It could hardly be expected of Thoreau's sister to sympathize with such a tribunal, especially when the same clear judgment was brought to bear upon the letters.

Even touching the contract for publication he was equally painstaking—far more so than for his own affairs. He wrote, "I inclose the first form of contract, as you requested, with the alterations suggested by Miss Thoreau." After this follows a careful reiteration in his own handwriting of such alterations as were desired. The early loss of Thoreau and his love for him were the root and flower which brought forth fruit in his noble discourse on "Immortality." Happy were they who heard him deliver those words, of which the printed page preserves the body, but the spirit with which it was delivered can not be reproduced! He wrote, the day after Thoreau's death, to Mr. Fields: "Come to-morrow and bring —— to my house. We will give you a very early dinner. Mr. Channing is to write a hymn or dirge for the funeral, which is to be from the church at three o'clock. I am to make an address, and probably Mr. Alcott may say something." This was the only announcement, the only time for preparation. Thoreau's body lay in the porch, and his town's-people filled the church, but Emerson made the simple ceremony one never to be forgotten by those who were present. Respecting the publication of this address I find the following entry in a diary of the time: "We have been waiting for Mr. Emerson to publish his new volume, containing his address upon Henry Thoreau; but he is careful of words, and finds many to be considered again and again, until it is almost impossible to extort a manuscript from his hands."

There is a brief note among the few letters I have found, respecting the poetry of some other writer whose name does not appear, but in the publication of whose work Emerson was evidently interested. He writes: "I have made the fewest changes

I could. So do not shock the *amour propre* of the poet, and yet strike out the bad words. You must, please, if it comes to question, keep my agency out of sight, and he will easily persuade himself that your compositor has grown critical, and struck out the rough syllables."

Emerson stood, as it were, the champion of American letters, and whatever found notice at all challenged his serious scrutiny. The soul and purpose must be there; he must find one line to win his sympathy, and then it was given with a whole heart. He said one day at breakfast that he had found a young man! A youth in the far West had written him, and enclosed some verses, asking for his criticism. Among them was the following line, which Emerson said proved him to be a poet, and he should watch his career in future with interest:

Life is a flame whose splendor hides the base.

We can imagine the kindly letter which answered the appeal, and how the future of that youth was brightened by it. "Emerson's young man" was a constant joke among his friends, because he was constantly filled with a large hope; and his friend of the one line was not by any means his only discovery.

His feeling respecting the literary work of men nearer to him was not always one of satisfaction. When Hawthorne's volume of *English Sketches* was printed, he said, "It is pellucid, but not deep"; and he cut out the dedication and letter to Franklin Pierce, which offended him. The two men were so unlike that it seemed a strange fate which brought them together in one small town. An understanding of each other's methods or points of view was an impossibility. Emerson spoke once with an intimate friend of the distance which separated Hawthorne and himself. They utterly disagreed upon politics and every theory of life.

Mr. Fields was suggesting to Emerson one day that he should give a series of lectures, when, as they were discussing the topics to be chosen, Emerson said: "One shall be on the 'Doctrine of Leasts,' and one on the 'Doctrine of Mosts'; one shall be about Brook Farm, for ever since Hawthorne's ghastly and untrue account of that community, in his *Blithedale Romance,* I have desired to give what I think the true account of it."

Sometimes, also, he had keen discussions and differences with Henry James. One day he appeared shocked at some of the doctrines advanced by Mr. James, and the conversation was dying, when Emerson's sister, who was present, took a chair, and planting it directly in front of James, said, "Let me confront the monster"; whereupon the topic was resumed, and they parted great friends.

He had many reservations also with regard to Dickens. He could not easily forgive any one who made him laugh immoderately. The first reading of *Dr. Marigold* in Boston was an exciting occasion, and Emerson was invited to assist. After the reading he sat talking until a very late hour, for he was taken by surprise at the novelty and artistic perfection of the performance. His usual calm had quite broken down under it; he had laughed as if he might crumble to pieces, his face wearing an expression of absolute pain; indeed, the scene was so strange that it was mirth-provoking to those who were near. But when we returned home he questioned and pondered much upon Dickens himself. Finally he said: "I am afraid he has too much talent for his genius; it is a fearful locomotive to which he is bound, and he can never be freed from it nor set at rest. You see him quite wrong evidently, and would persuade me that he is a genial creature, full of sweetness and amenities, and superior to his talents; but I fear he is harnessed to them. He is too consummate an artist to have a thread of nature left. He daunts me. I have not the key." When Mr. Fields came in he repeated: "—— would persuade me that Dickens is a man easy to communicate with, sympathetic and accessible to his friends; but her eyes do not see clearly in this matter, I am sure!"

On the other hand, the tenor of his way was largely stayed by admiration and appreciation of others, often far beyond their worth. He gilded his friends with his own sunshine. He wrote to his publisher: "Give me leave to make you acquainted with ——" (still unknown to fame), "who has written a poem which he now thinks of publishing. It is, in my judgment, a serious and original work of great and various merit, with high intellectual power in accosting the questions of modern thought, full of noble sentiment, and especially rich in fancy, and in sensibility to natural beauty. I remember that while reading it I thought it a welcome proof, and still more a prediction, of American culture. I need not trouble you with any cavils I made on the manuscript I read, as —— assures me that he has lately revised and improved the original draft. I hope you will like the poem as heartily as I did."

I find a record of one very warm day in Boston in July when, in spite of the heat, Mr. Emerson came to dine with us:

He talked much of Forceythe Willson, whose genius he thought akin to Dante's, and says E—— H—— agrees with him in this, or possibly suggested it, she having been one of the best readers and lovers of Dante outside the reputed scholars. "But he is not fertile. A man at his time should be doing new things." "Yes," said ——, "I fear he never will do much more." "Why, how old is he?" asked Emerson; and hearing he was about thirty-five, he replied, with a smile, "There is hope till forty-five." He spoke also of Tennyson and Carlyle as the two men connected with literature in England who were most satisfactory to meet, and better than their books. His respect for literature in these degenerate days is absolute. It is religion and life, and he reiterates this in every possible form. Speaking of Jones Very, he said he seemed to have no right to his rhymes; they did not sing to him, but he was divinely led to them, and they always surprised you.

We were much pleased and amused at his quaint expressions of admiration for a mutual friend in New York at whose hospitable house we had all received cordial entertainment. He said: "The great Hindoo, Hātim Tayi, was nothing by the side of such hospitality as hers. Hātim Tayi would soon lose his reputation." His appreciation of the poems of H. H. was often expressed. He made her the keynote of a talk one day upon the poetry of women. The poems entitled "Joy," "Thought," "Ariadne," he liked especially. Of Mrs. Hemans he found many poems which still survive, and he believed must always live.

Matthew Arnold was one of the minds and men to whom he constantly reverted with pleasure. Every traveler was asked for the last news of him, and when an English professor connected with the same university as Arnold, whom Emerson had been invited to meet, was asked the inevitable question, and found to know nothing, Emerson turned away from him, and lost all interest in his conversation. A few days afterward some one was heard to say, "Mr. Emerson, how did you like Professor ——?"

"Let me see," he replied; "is not he the man who was at the same university with Matthew Arnold, and who could tell us nothing of him?"

"How about Matthew Arnold?" he said to B—— on his return from England.

"I did not see him," was the somewhat cool reply.

"Yes! but he is one of the men one wishes not to lose sight of," said Emerson.

"Arnold has written a few good essays," rejoined the other, "but his talk about Homer is all nonsense."

"No, no, no!" said Emerson; "it is good, every word of it!"

When the lecture on Brook Farm really came, it was full of wit and charm, as well as of the truth he so seriously desired to convey. The audience was like a firm, elastic wall, against which he threw the balls of his wit, while they bounded prettily back into his hand. Almost the first thing he said was quoted from Horatio Greenough, whom he esteemed one of the greatest men of our country. But there is nothing more elusive and difficult to retain than Emerson's wit. It pierces and is gone. Some of the broader touches, such as the clothespins dropping out of the pockets of the Brook Farm gentlemen as they danced in the evening, were apparent to all, and irresistible. Nothing could be more amusing than the boyish pettishness with which, in speaking of the rareness of best company, he said, "We often found ourselves left to the society of cats and fools."

Emerson was always faithful to his appreciation of Channing's poems. When "Monadnock" was written, he made a special visit to Boston to talk it over, and the fine lines of Channing were always ready in his memory, to come to the front when called for. His love and loyalty to Elizabeth Hoar should never be forgotten in however imperfect a rehearsal of his valued companionships. One morning at breakfast I heard him describing her attributes and personality in the most tender and engaging way to Mrs. Stowe, who had never known her, which I would give much to be able to reproduce.

Emerson's truthfulness was often the cause of mirth even to himself. I remember that he thought he did not care for the work of Bayard Taylor, but he confessed one day with sly ruefulness that he had taken up the last *Atlantic* by chance, and found there some noble hexameters upon "November," and "I said to myself, 'Ah! who is this? this is as good as Clough.' When to my astonishment, and not a little to my discomfiture, I discovered they were Bayard Taylor's! But how about this 'Faust'? We have had Dante done over and over, and even now done I see again by a new hand, and Homer forever being done, and now 'Faust'! I quarrel somewhat with the over-much labor spent upon these translations, but first of all I quarrel with Goethe. 'Faust' is unpleasant to me. The very flavor of the poem repels me, and makes me wish to turn away." The *Divina Commedia,* too, he continued, was a poem too terrible to him to read. He had never been able to finish it. It is probable that poor translations of both 'Faust' and Dante read in early youth were at the bottom of these opinions.

Emerson was a true appreciator of Walter Scott. At one of the Saturday Club dinners it was suggested that Walter Scott be made the subject of conversation, and the occasion be considered as his birthday. Emerson spoke with brilliant effect two or three times. He was first called out by his friend Judge Hoar, who said he was chopping wood that morning in his woodshed, when Emerson came in and said so many delightful things about Sir Walter that if he would now repeat to the table only a portion of the excellent sayings heard in the woodshed he would delight them all. Emerson rose, and, referring pleasantly to the brilliancy of the judge's imagination, began by expressing his sense of gratitude to Walter Scott, and concluded a fine analysis of his work by saying that the root and gist of his genius was to be found, in his opinion, in the Border Minstrelsy.

Emerson was no lover of the sentimental school. The sharp arrow of his wit found a legitimate target there. Of one person in especial, whom we all knew and valued for extraordinary gifts, he said: "—— is irreclaimable. The sentimentalists are the most dangerous of the insane, for they can not be shut up in asylums."

The labor bestowed upon his own work before committing himself to print was limitless. I have referred to this already in speaking of the publication of his address after the death of Thoreau. Sometimes in joke a household committee would be formed to sit in judgment on his essays, and get them out of his hands. The "May-day" poem was long in reaching its home in print. There were references to it from year to year, but he could never be satisfied to yield it up. In April, 1865, after the fall of Richmond, he dined with us, full of what he said was "a great joy to the world, not alone to our little America." That day he brought what he then called some verses on spring to read to us, but when the reading was ended, he said they were far "too fragmentary to satisfy him," and quietly folded them up and carried them away again.

This feeling of unreadiness to print sprang as much from the wonderful modesty as from the sincerity of his character. He wrote shortly after to his publisher:

I have the more delight in your marked overestimate of my poem that I had been vexed with a belief that what skill I had in whistling was nearly or quite gone, and that I might henceforth content myself with guttural consonants or dissonants, and not attempt warbling. On the strength of your note, I am working away at my last pages of rhyme. But this has been and is a week of company. Yet I shall do the best I can with the quarters of hours.

Again, with his mind upon the "May-day" poem, he wrote:

I have long seen with some terror the necessity closing round me, in spite of all my resistance, that shall hold me from home. It now seems fixed to the 20th or 21st March. I had only consented to 1st March. But in the negotiations of my agent it would still turn out that the primary engagements made a year ago, and to which the others were only appendages—the primaries, St. Louis, Cincinnati, and Pittsburgh —must needs thrust themselves into March, and without remedy. But I can not allow the "May-day" to come till I come. There were a few indispensable corrections made and sent to the printer, which he reserved to be corrected on the plates, but of which no revise was ever sent to me; and as good publish no book as leave these *errata* unexpunged. Then there is one quatrain, to which his notice was not called, for which I wish to substitute another. So I entreat you not to finish the book except for the fire until I come. As the public did not die for the book on the 1st January, I presume they can sustain its absence on the 1st April. . . . Though I do not know that your courage will really hold out to publish it on the 1st April if I were quite ready.

Again in the same spirit he writes to his editor and publisher:

You ask in your last note for "Leasts and Mosts" for the *Atlantic*. You have made me so popular by your brilliant advertising and arrangements (I will say, not knowing how to qualify your social skill) that I am daily receiving invitations to read lectures far and near, and some of these I accept, and must therefore keep the readable lectures by me for a time, though I doubt not that this mite, like the mountain, will fall into the *Atlantic* at last.

> Ever your debtor,
> R. W. EMERSON

At another time he wrote:

I received the account rendered of the Blue and Gold Edition of the *Essays* and *Poems*. I keep the paper before me, and study it now and then to see if you have lost money by the transaction, and my prevailing impression is that you have.

It was seldom he showed a sincere willingness or desire to print. One day, however (it was in 1863), he came in bringing a poem he had written concerning his elder brother, who, he said, was a rare man, and whose memory richly deserved some tribute. He did not know if he could finish it, but he would like to print *that*. It was about the same period that he came to town and took a room at the Parker House, bringing with him the unfinished sketch of a few verses which he wished Mr. Fields to hear. He drew a small table into the center of the room, which was still in disorder (a former occupant having slept there the previous night), and then read aloud the lines he proposed to give to the press. They were written on separate slips of paper, which were flying loosely about the room and under the bed. A question arose of the title, when Mr. Fields suggested "Voluntaries," which was cordially accepted and finally adopted.

He was ever seeking suggestions, and ready to accept corrections. He wrote to his publisher:

I thank you for both the corrections, and accept them both, though in reading, one would always say, "You pet," so please write, though I grudge it, [Thou pet], and [mass], and [minster]. Please also to write [arctic] in the second line with small [a] if, as I think, it is now written large [A]. And I forgot, I believe, to strike out a needless series of quotation commas with which the printing was encumbered.

His painstaking never relaxed, even when he was to read a familiar lecture to an uncritical audience. He had been invited by the members of the Young Ladies' Saturday Morning Club to read one of his essays in their parlor. This he kindly consented to do, as well as to pass the previous night with his friends in Charles Street, and read to them an unpublished paper, which he called "Anita." Some question having arisen as to the possibility of his keeping both the engagements, he wrote as follows:

Dear Mrs. F.,
—I mean surely to obey your first command, namely, for the visit to you on Friday evening next, and I fully trust that I wrote you that I would. . . . And now I will untie the papers of "Anita," and see if I dare read them on Friday, or must find somewhat less nervous.

I find the following brief record of the occasion:

Mr. Emerson arrived from Concord. He said he took it for granted we should be occupied at that hour, but he would seize the moment to look over his papers. So I begged him to go into the small study and find quiet there as long as he chose. . . . Presently Emerson came down to tea; the curtains were drawn, and a few guests arrived. We sat round the tea table in the library, while he told us of ——'s life in Berlin, where Mr. and Mrs. Hermann Grimm and Mr. and Mrs. Bancroft had opened a pleasant social circle for him. He also talked much of the Grimms. His friendship for Hermann Grimm had extended over many years, and an interesting correspondence has grown up between them. More guests arrived, and the talk became general until the time came to listen to "Anita."

This is not the place to speak of the charm of that reading. The paper given that night is soon to be published, and as much of it as can be found on the printed page will be widely read and enjoyed; but Emerson's enjoyment of his own wit, as reflected back from the faces of his listeners, can not be reproduced, nor a kind of squirrel-like shyness and swiftness which pervaded it.

The diary continues:

C—— and —— were first at breakfast, but Mr. Emerson soon followed. The latter had been some time at work, and his hands were cold. I had heard him stirring before seven o'clock. He came down bright and fresh, however, with the very spirit of youth in his face. At table they fell upon that unfailing resource in conversation, anecdotes of animals and birds. Speaking of parrots, Mr. Emerson said he had never heard a parrot say any of these wonderful things himself, but the Storer family of Cambridge, who were very truthful people, had told him astonishing anecdotes of a bird belonging to them, which he could not disbelieve because they told him!

At ten o'clock we went to Miss L——'s, where the young ladies' club was convened to hear Mr. Emerson on "Manners." He told us we should do better to stay at home, as we had heard this paper many times. Happily we did not take his advice. There were many good things added besides the pleasure of hearing the old ones revived. One of the things new to me was the saying of a wise woman, who remarked that she "did not think so much of what people said as of what made them say it." It was pretty to see the enthusiasm of the girls, and to hear what C—— T—— called their "virile applause."

During the same season Emerson consented to give a series of readings in Boston. He was not easily persuaded to the undertaking until he felt assured of the very hearty cooperation which the proposed title of "Conversations" made evident to him. The following note will give some idea of his feeling with regard to the plan.

Concord, 24th February, 1872

Dear ——,

—You are always offering me kindness and eminent privileges, and for this courageous proposition of "Conversations on Literature with Friends, at Mechanics' Hall," I pause and poise between pleasure and fear. The name and the undertaking are most attractive; but whether it can be adequately attempted by me, who have a couple of tasks which Osgood and Company know of, now on my slow hands, I hesitate to affirm. Well, the very proposal will perhaps arm my head and hands to drive these tasks to a completion. And you shall give me a few days' grace, and I will endeavor to send you a considerate answer.

Later, in March, he wrote:

For the proposed "Conversations," which is a very good name, I believe I must accept your proposition frankly, though the second week of April looks almost too near.

As the appointed time approached, a fresh subject for nervousness suggested itself, which the following note will explain:

Concord, 12th April, 1872

My dear ——

—I entreat you to find the correspondent of the New York *Tribune,* ——, . . . who reports Miss Vaughan's and Henry James's lectures in Boston, . . . and adjure her or him, as he or she values honesty and honor, not to report any of what Mr. Emerson may say or do at his coming "Conversations." Tell the dangerous person that Mr. E. accepted this task, proffered to him by private friends, on the assurance that the audience would be composed of his usual circle of private friends, and that he should be protected from any report; that a report is so distasteful to him that it would seriously embarrass and perhaps cripple or silence much that he proposes to communicate; and if the individual has bought tickets, these shall gladly be refunded, and with thanks and great honor of your friend,

R. W. EMERSON

In spite of all these terrors, the "Conversations" were an entire success, financially as well as otherwise.

I find in the diary:

This afternoon Mr. Emerson gave his first "Conversation" in this course, which —— has arranged for him. He will make over fourteen hundred dollars by these readings. There was much new and excellent matter in the discourse today, and it was sown, as usual, with felicitous quotations. His introduction was gracefully done. He said he regarded the company around him as a society of friends whom it was a great pleasure to him to meet. He spoke of the value of literature, but also of the superior value of thought if it can be evolved in other ways, quoting that old saying of Catherine de Medicis, who remarked, when she was told of some one who could speak twenty languages: "That means he has twenty words for one idea. I would rather have twenty ideas to one word."

And again:

April 22.—Today is the second of Mr. Emerson's "Readings," or "Conversations," and he is coming with Longfellow and the Hunts to have dinner afterward. . . . We had a gay, lovely time at dinner; but— first about the lecture. Emerson talked of poetry, and the unity which exists between science and poetry, the latter being the fine insight which solves all problems. The *un*written poetry of today, the virgin soil, was strongly, inspiringly, revealed to us. He was not talking, he said, when he spoke of poetry, of the smooth verses of magazines, but of poetry itself wherever it was found. He read favorite single lines, also, from Byron's "Island," giving Byron great praise, as if in view of the injustice which has been done him in our time. After Byron's poem he read a lyric written by a traveler to the Tonga Islands, which is in Martin's *Travels;* also a noble poem called "The Soul," and a sonnet, by Wordsworth. We were all entranced as the magic of his sympathetic voice passed from one poetic vision to another. Indeed, we could not bear to see the hour fade away.

I find the following fragment of a note written during May of that year:

I received on my return home last night, with pleasure which is quite ceasing to surprise, the final installment of one hundred and seven dollars from the singular soliloquies called "Conversations," inaugurated by the best of directors.

Evermore thanks,
R. W. EMERSON

Again, in the journal I find:

Another lecture from Emerson—"Poetry, Religion, Love"—*"superna respicit amor."* His whole discourse was a storehouse of delights and inspirations. There was a fine contribution from Goethe; a passage where he bravely recounts his indebtedness to the great of all ages.

Varnhagen von Ense, Jacob Böhmen, Swedenborg, and the poets brought their share.

There was an interlude upon domestic life, "where alone the true man could be revealed," which was full of beauty.

He came in today to see ——. He flouts the idea of "that preacher, Horace Greeley," being put up for candidate for President. "If it had been Charles Francis Adams, now, we should all have voted for him. To be sure, it would be his father and his grandfather for whom we were voting, but we should all believe in him."

We think this present course of lectures more satisfactory than the last. One thing is certain, he flings his whole spirit into them. He reads the poems he loves best in literature, and infuses into their rendering the pure essence of his own poetic life. We can never forget his reading of "The Wind," a Welsh poem by Taliesin—the very rush of the elements was in it.

Emerson was perfectly natural and at ease in manner and speech during these readings. He would sometimes bend his brows and shut his eyes, endeavoring to recall a favorite passage, as if he were at his own library table. One day, after searching thus in vain for a passage from Ben Jonson, he said: "It is all the more provoking as I do not doubt many a friend here might help me out with it."

When away from home, on his lecture tours, Emerson did not fail to have his share of disasters. He wrote from Albany, in 1865, to Mr. Fields:

An unlucky accident drives me here to make a draft on you for fifty dollars, which I hope will not annoy you. The truth is that I lost my wallet—I fear to some pickpocket—in Fairhaven, Vermont, night before last (some $70 or $80 in it), and had to borrow money of a Samaritan lady to come here. I pray you do not whisper it to the swallows for fear it should go to ——, and he should print it in *Fraser*. I am going instantly to the best bookshop to find some correspondent of yours to make me good. I was to have read a lecture here last night, but the train *walked* all the way through the ice, sixty miles, from six in the morning, and arrived here at *ten* at night. I hope still that Albany will entreat me on its knees to read to-night. One other piece of bad news, if you have not already learned it. Can you not burn down the Boston Athenaeum to-night? for I learned by chance that they have a duplicate of the *Liber Amoris*. I hope for great prosperity on my journey as the necessary recoil of such adversities, and specially to pay my debts in twenty days.

Yours, with constant regard,
R. W. EMERSON

The apprehensions which assailed him before his public addresses or readings were not of a kind to affect either speech or behavior. He seemed to be simply detained by his own dissatisfaction with his work, and was forever looking for something better to come, even when it was too late. His manuscripts were often disordered, and at the last moment, after he began to read, appeared to take the form in his mind of a forgotten labyrinth through which he must wait to find his way in some more opportune season.

In the summer of 1867 he delivered the address before the Phi Beta at Harvard. He seemed to have an especial feeling of unreadiness on that day, and, to increase the trouble, his papers slipped away in confusion from under his hand as he tried to rest them on a poorly arranged desk or table. Mr. Hale put a cushion beneath them finally, after Emerson began to read, which prevented them from falling again, but the whole matter was evidently out of joint in the reader's eyes. He could not be content with it, and closed without warming to the occasion. It was otherwise, however, to those who listened; they did not miss the old power; but after the reading he openly expressed his own discontent, and walked away dissatisfied.

On another and more private occasion, also, he came away much disappointed himself, because, the light being poor and his manuscript disarranged, he had not been just, he thought, even to such matter as lay before him. And who can forget the occasion of the delivery of the Boston Hymn?—that glad New Year when the people were assembled in our large Music Hall to hear read the proclamation of Abraham Lincoln. When it was known that Emerson was to follow with a poem, a stillness fell on the vast assembly as if one ear were waiting to catch his voice; but the awful moment, which was never too great for his will and endeavor, was confusing to his fingers, and the precious leaves of his manuscript fell as he rose, and scattered themselves among the audience. They were quickly gathered and restored, but for one instant it seemed as if the cup so greatly desired was to be dashed from the lips of the listeners.

His perfect grace in conversation can hardly be reproduced, even if one could gather the arrows of his wit. But I find one or two slight hints of the latter which are too characteristic to be omitted. Speaking of some friends who were contemplating a visit to Europe just after our war, when exchange was still very high, he said that "the wily American would elude Europe for a year yet, hoping exchange would go down." On being introduced to an invited guest of the Saturday Club, Emerson said: "I am glad to meet you, sir. I often see your name in the papers, and elsewhere, and am happy to take you by the hand for the first time."

"Not for the first time," was the reply. "Thirty-three years ago I was enjoying my school vacation in the woods, as boys will. One afternoon I was walking alone, when you saw me and joined me, and talked of the voices of nature in a way which stirred my boyish pulses, and left me thinking of your words far into the night."

Emerson looked pleased, but rejoined that it must have been long ago indeed when he ventured to talk of such fine subjects.

In conversing with Richard H. Dana, Jr., the latter spoke of the cold eyes of one of our public men. "Yes," said Emerson, meditatively, "holes in his head! holes in his head!"

In speaking once of education and of the slight attention given to the development of personal influence, he said "he had not yet heard of Rarey" (the famous horse-tamer of that time) "having been made Doctor of Laws."

After an agreeable conversation with a gentleman who had suffered from ill health, Emerson remarked, "You formerly bragged of bad health, sir; I trust you are all right now."

Emerson's reticence with regard to Carlyle's strong expressions against America was equally wise and admirable. His friends crowded about him, urging him to denounce Carlyle, as a sacred duty, but he stood serene and silent as the rocks until the angry sea was calm.

Of his grace of manner, what could be more expressive than the following notes of compliment and acknowledgment?

When I came home from my pleasant visit to your house last week (or was it a day or two before last week?), Mrs. Hawthorne, arriving in Concord a little later than I, brought me the photograph of Raffaelle's original sketch of Dante, and from you. It appears to be a fixed idea in your mind to benefit and delight me, and still in ingenious and surprising ways. Well, I am glad that my lot is cast in the time and proximity of excellent persons, even if I do not often see their faces. I send my thanks for this interesting picture, which so strangely brings us close to the painter again, and, almost hints that a supermarine and superaerial telegraph may bring us thoughts from him yet.

And, again, with reference to a small photograph from a very interesting *rilievo* done by a young Roman who died early, leaving nothing in more permanent form to attest his genuis:

"The Star-led Wizards" arrived safely at my door last night, as the beauty and splendid fancy of their figures, and not less the generous instructions of their last entertainer and guide, might well warrant and secure.

It was surely a very unlooked-for but to me most friendly inspiration of yours which gave their feet this direction. But they are and shall be gratefully and reverently received and enshrined, and in the good hope that you will so feel engaged at some time or times to stop and make personal inquiry after the welfare of your guests and wards.

And again:

How do you suppose that unskillful scholars are to live, if Fields should one day die? *Serus in coelum redeat!*

Affectionately yours and his,

R. W. EMERSON

Surely the grace and friendly charm of these conversational notes warrant their preservation even to those who are not held by the personal attraction which lay behind them.

Again he writes:

I have been absent from home since the noble Saturday evening, or should have sent you this book of Mr. Stirling's, which you expressed a wish to see. The papers on Macaulay, Tennyson, and Coleridge interest me, and the critic is master of his weapons.

Meantime, in these days, my thoughts are all benedictions on the dwellers in the happy home of number 148 Charles Street.

His appreciation of the hospitality of others was only a reflection from his own. I find a few words in the journal as follows: "Mr. Emerson was like a benediction in the house, as usual. He was up early in the morning looking over books and pictures in the library." Afterward, in describing an evening when other guests were present, I find that he brought his own journal to town and read us passages describing a visit in Edinburgh, where he was the guest of Mrs. Crowe. She was one of those ladies of Edinburgh, he said, "who could turn to me, as she did, and say, 'Whom would you like to meet?' Of course I said, Lord Jeffrey, De Quincey, Samuel Brown, called the alchemist by chemists, and a few others. She was able, with her large hospitality, to give me what I most desired. She drove with me and Samuel Brown to call on De Quincey, who was then living most uncomfortably in lodgings with a landlady who persecuted him continually. While I was staying at Mrs. Crowe's, De Quincey arrived there one evening, after being exposed to various vicissitudes of weather, and latterly to a heavy rain. Unhappily Mrs. Crowe's apparently unlimited hospitality was limited at pantaloons, and poor De Quincey was obliged to dry his water-soaked garments at the fire-side."

Emerson read much also that was interesting of Tennyson and of Carlyle. Of the latter he said that the last time he was in England he drove directly to his house. "Jane Carlyle opened the door for me, and the man himself stood behind and bore the candle. 'Well, here we are, shoveled together again,' was his greeting. Carlyles' talk is like a river, full and never ceasing; we talked until after midnight, and again the next morning at breakfast we went on. Then we started to walk to London; and London Bridge, the Tower, and Westminster were all melted down into the river of his speech."

After the reading that evening there was singing, and Emerson listened attentively. Presently he said, when the first song ended, "I should like to know what the words mean." The music evidently signified little to his ears. Before midnight, when we were alone, he again reverted to Tennyson. He loves to gather and rehearse what is known of that wonderful man.

Early in the morning he was once more in the library. I found him there laughing over a little book he had discovered. It was Leigh Hunt's copy of *English Traits,* and was full of marginal notes, which amused Emerson greatly.

Not Mrs. Crowe's hospitality nor any other could ever compare in his eyes with that of the New York friend to whom I have already alluded. We agreed that her genius was pre-eminent. Here are two brief notes of graceful acknowledgment to his Boston friends which, however, may hardly be omitted. In one of these he says:

My wife is very sensible of your brave hospitality, offered in your note a fortnight since, and resists all my attempts to defend your hearth from such a crowd. Of course I am too glad to be persuaded to come to you, and so it is our desire to spend the Sunday of my last lecture at your house.

In the other he says:

I ought to have acknowledged and thanked you for the plus-Arabian
hospitality which warms your note. It might tempt any one but a
galley-slave, or a scholar who is tied to his book-crib as the other to
his oar, to quit instantly all his dull surroundings, and fly to this lighted,
genial asylum with doors wide open and nailed back.

There is a brief glimpse of Emerson upon his return from California which it is a pleasure to recall. He came at once, even before
going to Concord, to see Mr. Fields. "We must not visit San
Francisco too young," he said, "or we shall never wish to come
away. It is called the 'Golden Gate' not because of its gold, but
because of the lovely golden flowers which at this season cover
the whole face of the country down to the edge of the great sea."
He smiled at the namby-pamby travelers who turned back because
of the discomforts of the trip into the valley of the Yosemite. It
was a place full of marvel and glory to him. The only regret at-
tending the trip seems to have been that he was obliged to miss
the meetings of the Saturday Club, which were always dear to him.
The following extract gives a picture of him about this time:

A call from Mr. Emerson, who talked of Lowell's "joyous genius."
He said: "I have read what he has done of late with great interest, and
am sorry to have been so slow as not to have written him yet, especially as I am to meet him at the club dinner today. How is Pope?" he
continued, crossing the room to look at an authentic portrait by Richardson of that great master of verse. "Such a face as this should send
us all to re-reading his works again." Then turning to the bust of
Tennyson, by Woolner, which stood near, he said, "The more I think
of this bust and the grand self-assertion in it, the more I like it." . . .
Emerson came in after the club dinner; Longfellow also. Mrs. G——
was present, and bragged grandly, and was very smart in talk. Afterward Emerson said he was reminded of Carlyle's expression with regard to Lady Duff Gordon, whom he considered a female St. Peter
walking fearlessly over the waves of the sea of humbug.

Opportunities for social communication were sacred in his eyes, and never to be lightly thrown aside. He wore an expectant look upon his face in company, as if waiting for some new word from the last comer. He was himself the stimulus, even when disguised as a listener, and his additions to the evenings called "Mr. Alcott's Conversations" were marked and eagerly expected. Upon the occasion of Longfellow's last departure for Europe in 1869, a private farewell dinner took place, where Emerson, Agassiz, Holmes, Lowell, Greene, Norton, Whipple, and Dana all assembled in token of their regard. Emerson tried to persuade Longfellow to go to Greece to look after the Klephs, the supposed authors of Romaic poetry, so beautiful in both their poetic eyes. Finding this idea unsuccessful, he next turned to the Nile, to those vast statues which still stand awful and speechless witnesses of the past. He was interesting and eloquent, but Longfellow was not to be persuaded. It was an excellent picture of the two contrasting characters—Longfellow, serene, considerate, with his plans arranged and his thought resting in his home and his children's requirements; Emerson, with eager, unresting thought, excited by the very idea of travel to plunge farther into the strange world where the thought of mankind was born.

This lover of hospitalities was also king in his own domain. In the winter of 1872 Mr. Fields was invited to read a lecture in Concord, and an early invitation came bidding us to pass the time under his rooftree. A few days before, however, a note came, saying that Emerson himself was detained in Washington, and could not reach home for the occasion. It was cold weather, and even the horse that carried us from the station to the house had on his winter coat; but roaring fires were blazing when we arrived, and were only less warm than our welcome.

After supper, when the lecture hour was approaching, I suddenly heard the front door open, and, before we could think, there was the dear sage himself ready with his welcome. He had lectured the previous evening in Washington, and left in the earliest possible train, coming through without pause to Concord. In spite of the snow and cold, he said he should walk to the lecture room as soon as he had taken a cup of tea, and before the opening sentence was concluded his welcome face appeared punctually at the door.

After the lecture the old house presented a cheerful countenance. Again the fires blazed, friends sent flowers, and Mr. Alcott joined in conversation. "Quite swayed out of his habit," said Emerson, "by the good cheer." The spirit of hospitality led the master of the house to be swayed also, for it was midnight before the talk was ended. It was wonderful to see how strong and cheerful and unwearied he appeared after his long journey. "I would not discourage this young acolyte," he said, turning to the lecturer of the evening and laughing, "by showing any sense of discomfort."

When we arose the next morning the sun was just dawning over the level fields of snow. The air was fresh, the sky cloudless, the glory of the scene indescribable. The weight of weariness I had brought from the city was lifted by the scene before me, and by the influence of the great nature who was befriending us within the four walls. It was good to look upon the landscape which was the source of his own inspirations.

Emerson was already in the breakfast room at eight o'clock. There was much talk about the lack of education in English literature among our young people. Emerson said a Boston man who usually appeared sufficiently well informed asked him if he had ever known Spinoza. He talked also of Walt Whitman and Coventry Patmore, and asked the last news of Allingham: when suddenly, as it seemed, the little horse came again in his winter coat, and carried us to the station, and that day was done.

There is a bit of description of Emerson as he appeared at a political meeting in his earlier years which I love to remember.

The meeting was called in opposition to Daniel Webster, and Emerson was to address the people. It was in Cambridgeport. When he rose to speak he was greeted by hisses, long and full of hate, but a friend said, who saw him there, that she could think of nothing but dogs baying at the moon. He was serene as moonlight itself.

But the days came when desire must fail, and the end draw near. One morning he wrote from Concord: "I am grown so old that, though I can read from a paper, I am no longer fit for conversation, and dare not make visits. So we send you our thanks, and you shall not expect us."

It has been a pleasure to rehearse in my memory these glimpses of Emerson, and, covered with imperfections as they are, I have found courage for welding them together in the thought that many minds must know him through his work who long to ask what he was like in his habit as he lived, and whose joy in their teacher can only be enhanced by such pictures as they can obtain of the righteousness and beauty of his personal behavior.

OLIVER WENDELL HOLMES

✪

Emerson—A Retrospect

Emerson's earthly existence was in the estimate of his own philosophy so slight an occurrence in his career of being that his relations to the accidents of time and space seem quite secondary matters to one who has been long living in the companionship of his thought. Still, he had to be born, to take in his share of the atmosphere in which we are all immersed, to have dealings with the world of phenomena, and at length to let them all "soar and sing" as he left his earthly halfway house. It is natural and pardonable that we should like to know the details of the daily life which the men whom we admire have shared with common mortals, ourselves among the rest. But Emerson has said truly, "Great geniuses have the shortest biographies. Their cousins can tell you nothing about them. They lived in their writings, and so their home and street life was trivial and commonplace." . . .

From the numerous extracts I have given from Emerson's writ-

It would be easy to suggest that the witty, rationalistic Dr. Holmes never fathomed the great transcendentalist whose neighborhood he lived in for fifty years. It is true that his *Ralph Waldo Emerson* (1885) has its shortcomings. Yet it has something useful to say about Emerson's character if not about Emerson's ideas. Holmes had a shrewd eye, even when he directed it respectfully at Emerson. The final chapter of the book appears here in abridged form.

ings it may be hoped that the reader will have formed an idea for himself of the man and of the life which have been the subjects of these pages. But he may probably expect something like a portrait of the poet and moralist from the hand of his biographer, if the author of this memoir may borrow the name which will belong to a future and better equipped laborer in the same field. He may not unreasonably look for some general estimate of the lifework of the scholar and thinker of whom he has been reading. He will not be disposed to find fault with the writer of the memoir if he mentions many things which would seem very trivial but for the interest they borrow from the individual to whom they relate.

Emerson's personal appearance was that of a scholar, the descendant of scholars. He was tall and slender, with the complexion which is bred in the alcove and not in the open air. He used to tell his son Edward that he measured six feet in his shoes, but his son thinks he could hardly have straightened himself to that height in his later years. He was very light for a man of his stature. He got on the scales at Cheyenne, on his trip to California, comparing his weight with that of a lady of the party. A little while afterwards he asked of his fellow-traveler, Professor Thayer, "How much did I weigh? A hundred and forty?" "A hundred and forty and a half," was the answer. "Yes, yes, a hundred and forty and a half! That *half* I prize; it is an index of better things!"

Emerson's head was not such as Schopenhauer insists upon for a philosopher. He wore a hat measuring six and seven-eighths on the cephalometer used by hatters, which is equivalent to twenty-one inches and a quarter of circumference. The average size is from seven to seven and an eighth, so that his head was quite small in that dimension. It was long and narrow, but lofty, almost symmetrical, and of more nearly equal breadth in its anterior and posterior regions than many or most heads.

His shoulders sloped so much as to be commented upon for

this peculiarity by Mr. Gilfillan, and like "Ammon's great son," he carried one shoulder a little higher than the other. His face was thin, his nose somewhat accipitrine, casting a broad shadow; his mouth rather wide, well formed and well closed, carrying a question and an assertion in its finely finished curves; the lower lip a little prominent, the chin shapely and firm, as becomes the cornerstone of the countenance. His expression was calm, sedate, kindly, with that look of refinement, centering about the lips, which is rarely found in the male New Englander, unless the family features have been for two or three cultivated generations the battlefield and the playground of varied thoughts and complex emotions as well as the sensuous and nutritive port of entry. His whole look was irradiated by an ever active inquiring intelligence. His manner was noble and gracious. Few of our fellow-countrymen have had larger opportunities of seeing distinguished personages than our present minister at the Court of St. James. In a recent letter to myself, which I trust Mr. Lowell will pardon my quoting, he says of Emerson: "There was a majesty about him beyond all other men I have known, and he habitually dwelt in that ampler and diviner air to which most of us, if ever, only rise in spurts."

From members of his own immediate family I have derived some particulars relating to his personality and habits which are deserving of record.

His hair was brown, quite fine, and, till he was fifty, very thick. His eyes were of the "strongest and brightest blue." The member of the family who tells me this says: "My sister and I have looked for many years to see whether any one else had such absolutely blue eyes, and have never found them except in sea captains. I have seen three sea captains who had them."

He was not insensible to music, but his gift in that direction was very limited, if we may judge from this family story. When he was in college, and the singing master was gathering his pupils, Emerson presented himself, intending to learn to sing. The master received him, and when his turn came, said to him, "Chord!" "What?" said Emerson. "Chord! Chord! I tell you," repeated the master. "I don't know what you mean," said Emerson. "Why, sing! Sing a note." "So I made some kind of a noise, and the singing master said, 'That will do, sir. You need not come again.' "

Emerson's mode of living was very simple: coffee in the morning, tea in the evening, animal food by choice only once a day, wine only when with others using it, but always *pie* at breakfast. "It stood before him and was the first thing eaten." Ten o'clock was his bedtime, six his hour of rising until the last ten years of his life, when he rose at seven. Work or company sometimes led him to sit up late, and this he could do night after night. He never was hungry—could go any time from breakfast to tea without food and not know it, but was always ready for food when it was set before him.

He always walked from about four in the afternoon till teatime, and often longer when the day was fine, or he felt that he should work the better.

It is plain from his writings that Emerson was possessed all his life long with the idea of his constitutional infirmity and insufficiency. He hated invalidism, and had little patience with complaints about ill health, but in his poems, and once or twice in his letters to Carlyle, he expresses himself with freedom about his own bodily inheritance. In 1827, being then but twenty-four years old, he writes:

> I bear in youth the sad infirmities
> That use to undo the limb and sense of age.

Four years later:

> Has God on thee conferred
>   A bodily presence mean as Paul's,
> Yet made thee bearer of a word
>   Which sleepy nations as with trumpet calls?

and again, in the same year:

> Leave me, Fear, thy throbs are base,
> Trembling for the body's sake.

Almost forty years from the first of these dates we find him bewailing his inherited weakness of organization in "Terminus."

And in writing to Carlyle, he says: "You are of the Anakim and know nothing of the debility and postponement of the blonde constitution."

Again, "I am the victim of miscellany—miscellany of designs, vast debility and procrastination."

He thought too much of his bodily insufficiencies, which, it will be observed, he only refers to in his private correspondence, and in that seminudity of self-revelation which is the privilege of poetry. His presence was fine and impressive, and his muscular strength was enough to make him a rapid and enduring walker.

Emerson's voice had a great charm in conversation, as in the lecture room. It was never loud, never shrill, but singularly penetrating. He was apt to hesitate in the course of a sentence, so as to be sure of the exact word he wanted; picking his way through his vocabulary, to get at the best expression of his thought, as a well-dressed woman crosses the muddy pavement to reach the opposite sidewalk. It was this natural slight and not unpleasant semicolon pausing of the memory which grew upon him in his years of decline, until it rendered conversation laborious and painful to him.

He never laughed loudly. When he laughed it was under protest, as it were, with closed doors, his mouth shut, so that the explosion had to seek another respiratory channel, and found its way out quietly, while his eyebrows and nostrils and all his features betrayed the "ground swell," as Professor Thayer happily called it, of the half-suppressed convulsion. He was averse to loud laughter in others, and objected to Margaret Fuller that she made him laugh too much.

Emerson was not rich in some of those natural gifts which are considered the birthright of the New Englander. He had not the mechanical turn of the whittling Yankee. I once questioned him about his manual dexterity, and he told me he could split a shingle four ways with one nail—which, as the intention is not to split it at all in fastening it to the roof of a house or elsewhere, I took to be a confession of inaptitude for mechanical works. He does not seem to have been very accomplished in the handling of agricultural implements either, for it is told in the family that his little son, Waldo, seeing him at work with a spade, cried out, "Take care, papa—you will dig your leg."

He used to regret that he had no ear for music. I have said enough about his verse, which often jars on a sensitive ear, showing a want of the nicest perception of harmonies and discords in the arrangement of the words.

There are stories which show that Emerson had a retentive memory in the earlier part of his life. It is hard to say from his books whether he had or not, for he jotted down such a multitude of things in his diary that this was a kind of mechanical memory which supplied him with endless materials of thought and subjects for his pen.

Lover and admirer of Plato as Emerson was, the doors of the academy, over which was the inscription μηδείς ἀγεωμέτρητος ἔσειτω —Let no one unacquainted with geometry enter here—would have been closed to him. All the exact sciences found him an unwilling learner. He says of himself that he cannot multiply seven by twelve with impunity.

In an unpublished manuscript kindly submitted to me by Mr. Frothingham, Emerson is reported as saying, "God has given me the seeing eye, but not the working hand." His gift was insight:

he saw the germ through its envelope; the particular in the light of the universal; the fact in connection with the principle; the phenomenon as related to the law; all this not by the slow and sure process of science, but by the sudden and searching flashes of imaginative double vision. He had neither the patience nor the method of the inductive reasoner; he passed from one thought to another not by logical steps but by airy flights, which left no footprints. This mode of intellectual action when found united with natural sagacity becomes poetry, philosophy, wisdom, or prophecy in its various forms of manifestation. Without that gift of natural sagacity (*odoratio quoedam venatica*)—a good scent for truth and beauty—it appears as extravagance, whimsicality, eccentricity, or insanity, according to its degree of aberration. Emerson was eminently sane for an idealist. He carried the same sagacity into the ideal world that Franklin showed in the affairs of common life.

He was constitutionally fastidious, and had to school himself to become able to put up with the terrible inflictions of uncongenial fellowships. We must go to his poems to get at his weaknesses. The clown of the first edition of "Monadnoc" "with heart of cat and eyes of bug," disappears in the afterthought of the later version of the poem, but the eye that recognized him and the nature that recoiled from him were there still. What must he not have endured from the persecutions of small-minded worshipers who fastened upon him for the interminable period between the incoming and outgoing railroad train! He was a model of patience and good temper. We might have feared that he lacked the sensibility to make such intrusions and offences an annoyance. But when Mr. Frothingham gratifies the public with those most interesting personal recollections which I have had the privilege of looking over, it will be seen that his equanimity, admirable as it was, was not incapable of being disturbed, and that on rare occasions he could give way to the feeling which showed itself of old in the doom pronounced on the barren fig tree.

Of Emerson's affections, his home life and those tender poems in memory of his brothers and his son give all the evidence that could be asked or wished for. His friends were all who knew him, for none could be his enemy; and his simple graciousness of manner, with the sincerity apparent in every look and tone, hardly admitted indifference on the part of any who met him, were it but for a single hour. Even the little children knew and loved him, and babes in arms returned his angelic smile. Of the friends who were longest and most intimately associated with him, it is needless to say much in this place. Of those who are living, it is hardly time to speak; of those who are dead, much has already been written. Margaret Fuller—I must call my early schoolmate as I best remember her—leaves her life pictured in the mosaic of five artists— Emerson himself among the number; Thoreau is faithfully commemorated in the loving memoir by Mr. Sanborn; Theodore Parker lives in the story of his life told by the eloquent Mr. Weiss; Hawthorne awaits his portrait from the master hand of Mr. Lowell.

How nearly any friend, other than his brothers Edward and Charles, came to him, I cannot say, indeed I can hardly guess. That "majesty" Mr. Lowell speaks of always seemed to hedge him round like the divinity that doth hedge a king. What man was he who would lay his hand familiarly upon his shoulder and call him Waldo? No disciple of Father Mathew would be likely to do such a thing. There may have been such irreverent persons, but if any one had so ventured at the "Saturday Club," it would have produced a sensation like Brummel's "George, ring the bell," to the Prince Regent. His ideas of friendship, as of love, seem almost too exalted for our earthly conditions, and suggest the thought as do many others of his characteristics, that the spirit which animated his mortal frame had missed its way on the shining path to some brighter and better sphere of being.

Not so did Emerson appear among the plain working farmers of the village in which he lived. He was a good, unpretending fellow-citizen who put on no airs, who attended town meetings, took his part in useful measures, was no great hand at farming, but was esteemed and respected, and felt to be a principal source of attraction to Concord, for strangers came flocking to the place as if it held the tomb of Washington.

What was the errand on which he visited our earth—the message with which he came commissioned from the Infinite source of all life?

Every human soul leaves its port with sealed orders. These may be opened earlier or later on its voyage, but until they are opened no one can tell what is to be his course or to what harbor he is bound.

Emerson inherited the traditions of the Boston pulpit, such as they were, damaged, in the view of the prevailing sects of the country, perhaps by too long contact with the "Sons of Liberty," and their revolutionary notions. But the most "liberal" Boston pulpit still held to many doctrines, forms, and phrases open to the challenge of any independent thinker.

In the year 1832 this young priest, then a settled minister, "began," as was said of another—"to be about thirty years of age." He had opened his sealed orders and had read therein:

Thou shalt not profess that which thou dost not believe.

Thou shalt not heed the voice of man when it agrees not with the voice of God in thine own soul.

Thou shalt study and obey the laws of the Universe and they will be thy fellow-servants.

Thou shalt speak the truth as thou seest it, without fear, in the spirit of kindness to all thy fellow-creatures, dealing with the manifold interests of life and the typical characters of history.

Nature shall be to thee as a symbol. The life of the soul, in conscious union with the Infinite, shall be for thee the only real existence.

This pleasing show of an external world through which thou art passing is given thee to intrepret by the light which is in thee. Its least appearance is not unworthy of thy study. Let thy soul be open and thine eyes will reveal to thee beauty everywhere.

Go forth with thy message among thy fellow-creatures; teach them that they must trust themselves as guided by that inner light which dwells with the pure in heart, to whom it was promised of old that they shall see God.

Teach them that each generation begins the world afresh, in perfect freedom; that the present is not the prisoner of the past, but that today holds captive all yesterdays, to compare, to judge, to accept, to reject their teachings, as these are shown by its own morning's sun.

To thy fellow-countrymen thou shalt preach the gospel of the New World, that here, here in our America, is the home of man; that here is the promise of a new and more excellent social state than history has recorded.

Thy life shall be as thy teachings, brave, pure, truthful, beneficient, hopeful, cheerful, hospitable to all honest belief, all sincere thinkers, and active according to thy gifts and opportunities.

He was true to the orders he had received. Through doubts, troubles, privations, opposition, he would not

bate a jot
Of heart or hope, but still bear up and steer
Right onward.

All through the writings of Emerson the spirit of these orders manifests itself. His range of subjects is very wide, ascending to the highest sphere of spiritual contemplation, bordering on that "intense inane" where thought loses itself in breathless ecstasy, and stooping to the homeliest maxims of prudence and the everyday lessons of good manners. And all his work was done, not so much

As ever in his great Taskmaster's eye,

as in the ever-present sense of divine companionship.

He was called to sacrifice his living, his position, his intimacies, to a doubt, and he gave them all up without a murmur. He might have been an idol, and he broke his own pedestal to attack the idolatry which he saw all about him. He gave up a comparatively easy life for a toilsome and trying one; he accepted a precarious employment, which hardly kept him above poverty, rather than wear the golden padlock on his lips which has held fast the conscience of so many pulpit Chrysostoms. Instead of a volume or two of sermons, bridled with a text and harnessed with a confession of faith, he bequeathed us a long series of Discourses and Essays in which we know we have his honest thoughts, free from that professional bias which tends to make the pulpit teaching of the fairest-minded preacher follow a diagonal of two forces—the promptings of his personal and his ecclesiastical opinions.

Without a church or a pulpit, he soon had a congregation. It was largely made up of young persons of both sexes, young by nature, if not in years, who, tired of routine and formulae, and full of vague aspirations, found in his utterances the oracles they sought. To them, in the words of his friend and neighbor Mr. Alcott, he

Sang his full song of hope and lofty cheer.

Nor was it only for a few seasons that he drew his audiences of devout listeners around him. Another poet, his Concord neighbor, Mr. Sanborn, who listened to him many years after the first flush of novelty was over, felt the same enchantment, and recognized the same inspiring life in his words, which had thrilled the souls of those earlier listeners.

His was the task and his the lordly gift
Our eyes, our hearts, bent earthward, to uplift.

This was his power—to inspire others, to make life purer, loftier, calmer, brighter. Optimism is what the young want, and he could no more help taking the hopeful view of the universe and its future than Claude could help flooding his landscapes with sunshine. . . .

✪

Emerson—The Brahmin View

Mr. Chairman, Members of the Social Circle, Ladies and Gentlemen of Concord and from abroad: It is well that this day should be celebrated throughout our land, for the memory of Emerson deserves more than mere local honor. It is well, moreover, because the celebration is a virtual protest against the prevalent spirit of materialism and militarism. But here, in this doubly consecrated town, the celebration, as you, Mr. Chairman, have justly said, has special significance and appropriateness, and you will not disapprove of my citing, as accordant with your own words, those of your honored father, Mr. Emerson's near friend, the "incomparable citizen," as he called him, the spokesman of the town at Emerson's

Throughout much of his active life Emerson was a controversial character. After giving his Divinity School Address at Harvard in 1838, he was effectively barred from speaking on its campus for the next twenty-five years. Nevertheless, his essential nobility gradually became evident even to those who detested many of his ideas. After the Civil War he was accorded an almost universal respect. Even Brahmin Boston, the Boston of the Puritan aristocrats and hard-bitten conservatives, gave him his due. A century after his birth a celebration was held in nearby Concord marked by a number of speeches. One came from Professor Charles Eliot Norton of Harvard, son of Andrews Norton, once Emerson's harshest critic. The son delivered a eulogy of Emerson which is as respectful and admiring as anyone could wish. It is also, in its stuffiness, a noteworthy period piece. His address, untitled in the original, is reprinted from *The Centenary of the Birth of Ralph Waldo Emerson* (1903).

funeral, when he said, in his brief and heartfelt address on that occasion: "We, his neighbors and townsmen, feel that he was *ours*. He was descended from the founders of the town. He chose our village as the place where his lifelong work was to be done. It was to our fields and orchards that his presence gave such value; it was our streets in which the children looked up to him with love, and the elders with reverence. He was our ornament and pride." It is becoming, then, that you, members of the Social Circle to which Emerson belonged for many years, should, above all, commemorate this anniversary, and should ask others to celebrate it with you. I thank you for inviting me to take part in it.

"There are always in the world," says Plato, "a few inspired men whose acquaintance is beyond price." "I am in the habit of thinking," said Mr. Emerson, "that to every serious mind Providence sends from time to time five or six or seven teachers who are of the first importance to him in the lessons they have to impart. The highest of these not so much give particular knowledge, as they elevate by sentiment, and by their habitual grandeur of view."

And of these highest inspired men whose acquaintance is beyond price, and who elevate those who come into relations with them by sentiment and habitual grandeur of view, was Emerson himself. In modern times the influence of these men is diffused through their printed words, and they become teachers of first importance to many remote and unknown readers. Yet now, as in the days of Plato, personal acquaintance with them is beyond price. But the printed word is diuturnal, and the personal acquaintance transitory. For a little while the personality of these divine men, cherished in the memories of a few of their contemporaries, continues to have a twilight existence; but before long all who knew them face to face have gone from the world, and only hearsay and tradition concerning them remain.

It is an interesting and precious element of this commemorative occasion that so many are taking part in it who remember Mr. Emerson in life, and who bear in their hearts the image of his benignant presence. We, the elders, who held acquaintance with him to be priceless, and for whom he felt a kindly regard or even a friendly affection, can hardly do a better service for the younger generation than to give them, so far as may be possible, a faithful impression of the man himself, who exhibited in his daily walk and conversation a nature of ideal simplicity, dignity, and elevation.

Emerson was fortunate in the time and place of his birth. I doubt if there has ever been a community happier in its main conditions, moral and material, than that of Massachusetts during the early years of the last century. But it was essentially immature; it had not yet secured intellectual independence; its thought, its literature, its manners, its religion, were imported and derivative. Many men of vigorous character and abundant natural capacity were found in it; but there were few who possessed originality or depth of intellect; no poets, no philosophers, no thinkers in the highest sense were here; nor were there any deep founts of learning.

Into this fortunate, immature, intelligent, religious, hopeful community, Emerson was born; born of admirable parents, the children of a long line of well-bred ancestors. He was born good, with an inheritance of serious-mindedness, of an intellectual disposition, and of religious sentiment. He was also born a poet, and the advantages of place and time of his birth gave form and direction to his poetic genius. Its very originality, that which distinguishes and individualizes it, exhibits its native source.

The originality of genius is often a strange and perplexing phenomenon to the contemporaries of its possessor—nor is it always understood by the man himself. Contemporaries fail to recognize at once the poet as the seer who reveals to them their own imperfectly developed tendencies, and expresses for them their own mute sentiments; while the poet, familiar with the conditions in which he lives, and unconsciously shaped by them, may fail, for a time at least, to note the partial incompatibility between the traditional and customary order of things and the novel ideas revealed to his poetic vision.

So it was with Emerson. The mass of his contemporaries for a long while looked askance on him, and regarded his utterances with suspicion and disapproval. And he himself made a long trial of the old ways before he arrived at the conviction that he could not follow them, but must take the independent course dictated to him by his genius. He was already thirty years old when he came to full self-reliance. Before he was forty years old he had delivered his chief message. This was no systematic philosophy, no dogmatic doctrine, but an individual interpretation of the universe, and of the life of man as a part of the universe.

The essence of his spiritual teaching seems to me to be comprised in three fundamental articles—first, that of the Unity of Being in God and Man; second, that of the creation of the visible, material world by Mind, and of its being the symbol of the spiritual world; and third, that of the identity and universality of moral law in the spiritual and material universe. These truths are for him the basis of life, the substance of religion, and the meaning of the universe.

From the little circle of selfish interests in which our lives are mainly spent, Emerson lifts us into the great circles of the universe, from the meanness of personal and individual considerations into the sense of the large spiritual relations of even our common daily affairs, and makes us conscious partakers of the general life of the universe, part and parcel of its divine order. It is this that Matthew Arnold meant when he said so well that Emerson "is the friend and aider of those who live in the spirit." Holding nature, and man as a part of nature, to be but a symbol and external manifestation of the Eternal and Infinite Mind, omnipresent in the form

of the Universe, the source of its law by which it works always
toward perfection, he cannot but be the most absolute of optimists.
There is no pause in the flow of Being through the world; everything is in a state of flux, and the main course of the stream is always forward, from good to better.

> Through flood and sea and firmament,
> Through light, through life it forward flows.

But truth that has been spiritually discerned must be spiritually
interpreted. When he insists on the divinity in man, and bids him
trust himself, it is not to the selfish and arrogant that he speaks,
but to the man who is endeavoring after righteousness and who
keeps his soul open to the influences of the divine essence which is
its source. His optimism is the same with that of Ecclesiasticus:
"All the works of the Lord are good—so that a man cannot say
this is worse than that, for in him they shall all be approved." And
his teaching of self-confidence is taught not less by the same wise
man of old: "In every good work trust thine own soul, for this is
the keeping of the commandments." "The soul converses with
truths," said Emerson, "that have always been spoken in the
world."

Emerson was of that class of men, individuals of which, as he
says, appear at long intervals, eminently endowed with insight and
virtue, and manifesting in every relation and expression a latent
indefinable power, which is of a different and higher order than
any talent and which compels attention and respect. It is the power
of character, that is, of the highest form of the nature of the man.
It is this which determines ultimately the extent and the strength
of his influence. In a noble nature it exhibits itself in every expression.

And if I were called on to describe Emerson in a single phrase,
I should say that of all the men I have known he made the
strongest impression of consistent loftiness of character. This char-

acter was no less manifest in familiar social relations than in his public discourses. His superiority was evident in the natural simplicity of his manners and demeanor. Affectation, self-consciousness, parade, were impossible to him. His habitual bearing was of sweet gravity and reserve, in which was no aloofness, but a ready responsiveness to every claim of thought or word of another. He was not lavish of sympathy, but in case of need no sympathy was more comprehensive than his. He inspired affection and honor in every one who knew him. His presence raised the level of every company.

His essays on "Character," "Manners," and "Behavior" show how penetrating and clear had been his observation of the ways of men, and how wise his conclusions from it—but though many of the finer traits which he described found illustration in himself, yet the secret of his superiority is hardly disclosed in them. It resided, I believe, in the fact that he lived more in accord with the moral order of the soul than other men, more as one whose soul was always open to the influences of the divine spirit, however that spirit be defined. In this was the source of the serenity and elevation of his own spirit, and in it was also the source of that clear insight into the significance of common life and daily trivial affairs which his reflections upon them and his aphorisms concerning them display.

In 1870, after reading Emerson's volume entitled *Society and Solitude,* Carlyle wrote to him in well-chosen words: "It seems to me you are all your old self here, and something more. A calm insight, piercing to the very center; a beautiful sympathy, a beautiful epic humor; a soul peaceably irrefragable in this loud-jangling world, of which it sees the ugliness, but *notices* only the huge new opulences (still so anarchic); knows the electric telegraph, with all its vulgar botherations and impertinences, accurately for what it is, and ditto ditto the oldest eternal Theologies of men. All this belongs to the Highest Class of thought; and again seemed to me as, in several respects, the one perfectly *Human* Voice I had heard among my fellow-creatures for a long time. And then the 'style,' the treatment and expression—yes, it is inimitable, best—Emersonian throughout. . . . You have done *very well;* and many will know it ever better by degrees." The judgment of the friend is confirmed by that of the new generation.

My own relations with Emerson began after his position as poet and seer was established, not with the great public indeed, but with the best of his contemporaries. Twenty-five years younger than he, I felt at first a certain hesitancy and shyness in personal relations with him, not only because of the disparity of age, and the distinction of his place in the esteem of worthy men, but also because my father had been conspicuous in opposition to the drift of his teachings and had used language of severe condemnation of them. It seemed to me possible that Mr. Emerson, though too high-minded to feel resentment toward an upright and high-minded opponent, might yet incline to hold back from more than merely formal acquaintance with me. But I was mistaken. From the beginning of our intercourse he treated me with a simple graciousness and frank confidence that set me at ease with him, and quickened in me that affection and reverence which I have just spoken of his inspiring in every one who had the happiness of coming into close relation with him.

Thirty years ago this month I had the opportunity of seeing more of him, and of being in more constant relation with him than at any other time. He was returning with his daughter from his last visit to Europe, and I, with my family, was a fellow passenger on the steamer. There was no crowd on board; the vessel was not one of the swift Leviathans of today. We had long walks together on the deck; and in the evening, after the rest of the passengers had gone to their berths, he and I used to sit talking together for an hour or two, till eleven o'clock, when the lights were extinguished in the deserted cabin. The visit to Europe and to Egypt had been undertaken, as some of you will remember, at the urgency of friends, in the belief that a change of scene and interest would be serviceable to him after the shock which he had experienced from the burning of his house in the summer, and the depressed condition of health which had followed it. It had done him all the good that had been hoped for, and he now seemed in excellent health and spirits.

"It is rank blasphemy," said he one day, "to doubt anything in the universe; everything in life makes for good. The moral element in man supreme, is progressive. Man is always better than himself. The world is all for happiness, and is meant for the happy. It is always improving. Pain and sorrow are of no account as compared with the joy of living; if a man be overcome by them he violates the moral order."

"The universe is not a cheat; the beauty and the order of the external world are sufficient proof that the spiritual world is in accord with the hopes and instincts of man and nature for their own perfection."

"Order, goodness, God are the one everlasting, self-existent fact."

"I measure a man's intellectual sanity by his faith in immortality. A wise man's wish for life is in proportion to his wisdom."

He would not entertain for a moment the evidence of ruthlessness and disorder in nature, of perversion of the moral nature in men. His faith was superior to any apparent exceptions to his doctrine; all of them could be brought into accordance with it.

In our long evening talks he told me much of his early life. He was often in a mood of reminiscence, and in the retrospect all life lay fair behind him, like a pleasant landscape illumined by the slowly sinking sun. The sweetness and purity and elevation of his nature were manifest in his recollections, and his vision of the past was that not only of the poet, but of the good man who had gained from life the best it can afford. He returned over and over

again to the happiness of life and the joy of existence. He had
been very fortunate in his times.

The twenty-fifth of May, his seventieth birthday, was the last
day before the voyage ended. When I greeted him in the morning,
he replied with a pleasant semi-humorous smile, and with a blush
like a youth, "You are too good with all these kind words, but the
day is a melancholy one for me, for I count this seventieth birthday
as the close of youth!" He had been reading with great interest on
the voyage the quatrains of Omar Khayyám, and one of them may
have been lingering in his mind:

> Yet Oh! that Spring should vanish with the Rose!
> That Youth's sweet-scented manuscript should close!
> The nightingale that in the branches sang,
> Ah whence, and whither flown again, who knows?

But my thoughts fell back to his own *Terminus,* written ten
years before; not so much to its opening words, "It is time to
grow old," but rather to the verses with which it ends:

> As the bird trims her to the gale,
> I trim myself to the storm of time,
> I man the rudder, reef the sail,
> Obey the voice at eve obeyed at prime;
> Lowly faithful, banish fear,
> Right onward drive unharmed;
> The port, well worth the cruise, is near,
> And every wave is charmed.

One day, a day of rough waves and lowering skies, as we
walked the deck, he spoke of the stout hearts of the early mariners,
sailing the untracked seas. "How, in Heaven's name, did Columbus
get over?" as Clough asks. "Not so much of a wonder after all,"
said Emerson; "Columbus had his compass, and that was enough
for such a soul as his; there was the miracle of the magnet, the
witness of the divine spirit in nature, type of the eternal control
of matter by spirit, of fidelity to the unseen and the ideal. I always

carry with me a little compass," and taking it from his pocket, he added, "I like to hold the god in my hand."

He lived for nine years after his return home. Some of you remember his gently declining days. The evening mists steadily gathered about him, but while they gradually obscured the light of his mind, they were still suffused by the unquenched glow of his spirit. His sweetness, his faith never failed.

On the last occasion that I saw him at his own house his powers of recollection were imperfect, but his gracious benignity was unchanged. His talk had its old tone, though the intermittent thoughts sometimes failed to find perfect expression. As I was bidding him good-by at his hospitable door, his daughter, who proposed to go with me to the railroad station, urged him to accompany us. "No," said he, "no, my dear, my good friend whose name I cannot recall, has had quite enough of me today"; and then turning to me with a smile, as if to apologize for the seeming lack of courtesy in his inability to recall my name, he said in words and manner like his old self, "Strange that the kind Heavens should keep us upon earth after they have destroyed our connection with things!"

The last time I saw him was at the funeral of Longfellow on the twenty-sixth of March, just a month before his own death. He leaned on my arm as we walked through the path at Mt. Auburn behind the poet's coffin, and as we stood listening to the short service at the grave. He hardly seemed to belong to our actual life; he was present but yet remote; for him, too, "The port well worth the cruise was near."

If there be pathos in the record of these last days, there is no drop of bitterness in it. They were the peaceful ending of a happy life. "Enoch walked with God; and he was not, for God took him."

Emerson's fame is secure. The years will sift his work, but his true message and service were not for his own generation alone. It is not the founders of schools whose influence is the strongest and most lasting in the world, but rather that of teachers who lift and invigorate the souls of men by sentiment and habitual loftiness of view. Men draw strength and high resolve today, after seventeen centuries, from the desultory *Meditations* of Marcus Aurelius, and in long future time men seeking to elevate and liberate their souls will find help in the words and example in the character of Emerson.

JAY B. HUBBELL

✪

Emerson and the South

I trust that no admirer of Ralph Waldo Emerson will think me lacking in appreciation for one of the wisest and greatest American writers because I have chosen him to illustrate the extent to which sectional controversy prevented the New England writers from understanding the ante-bellum South. This, I am thoroughly aware, is to present Emerson at his worst. At the same time, although my story ends on a note of reconciliation, Southern critics of Emerson seem more lacking in insight than they were when they discussed the work of writers from New York and Pennsylvania.

Much that Emerson wrote about the South and slavery was at odds with some of his most characteristic ideas. This inconsistency did not disturb the Concord sage, but it may disturb some of his admirers. He once referred to abolitionists and other professional reformers as "an altogether odious set of people whom one would shun as the worst of bores and canters." The only way to make the

---

An unusual perspective on Emerson is offered us by a leading student of Southern literature, Professor Jay Hubbell. In his definitive *The South in American Literature* (1954) he describes Emerson's critical attitude toward the South and the South's toward him, but he does so judiciously, even urbanely. The section entitled "Ralph Waldo Emerson" is reprinted from his book with the permission of Professor Hubbell and Duke University Press. There is an enlarged and revised version in his *South and Southwest* (1965).

world better, he thought, was to make better the individuals in it, and he was echoing Jefferson when he said that "the less government we have the better,—the fewer laws, and the less confided power." It was useless to try to reform society by attacking a single abuse. In "New England Reformers" he said in 1844: "Do not be so vain of your one objection [to society]. Do you think there is only one? Alas! my good friend, there is no part of society or of life better than any other part. All our things are right and wrong together. The wave of evil washes all our institutions alike. Do you complain of our Marriage? Our marriage is no worse than our education, our diet, our trade, our social customs." Might he not logically have added: ". . . than African slavery on Southern plantations or industrial servitude in New England mills and factories"?

Soon after his graduation from Harvard in 1821 Emerson wrote to a friend in Baltimore: "You know our idea of an accomplished Southerner; to wit, as ignorant as a bear, as irascible and nettled as any porcupine, as polite as a troubadour, and a very John Randolph in character and address." Emerson's notion of the Southern character shows plainly some marks of the traditional New England conception, but it was based in part on an acquaintance with Southern students at Harvard. For a brief time he shared a room with a Charlestonian, John Gourdin, whom Dr. Holmes describes as showy and fascinating. The recognized leader of Emerson's class was another South Carolinian, Robert Woodward Barnwell, whom President Josiah Quincy remembered as the "first scholar of the class . . . a noble specimen of the Southerner, high-spirited, interesting, and a leader of men." We shall hear of Barnwell again.

Health-seekers from New England often went South to avoid the cold Northern winter. It was thus that Emerson, recently ordained as a minister, spent the winter of 1826–1827 in Charleston and St. Augustine. This journey into what he felt was a foreign country had no such determining influence as his European visit six years later. The verses he wrote and the entries in his *Journals* indicate that he thought of himself as an exile. The Catholic priests and the Methodist ministers whom he heard, or heard of, confirmed his low opinion of the state of religion in the South. He felt, however, no deep repulsion from slavery as yet. That, as with Dr. Channing, was to come some years after he had left the South. He did, however, note a certain incongruity between slavery and Christianity. In St. Augustine he wrote in the *Journals* that he had attended a meeting of a Bible society, of which the treasurer was the district marshal. By "a somewhat unfortunate arrangement" the treasurer had called a meeting of the society in the government house while a slave auction was being conducted just outside. "One ear therefore heard the glad tidings of great joy, whilst the other was regaled with 'Going, gentlemen, going!' And almost without changing our position we might aid in sending the Scriptures into Africa, or bid for 'four children without the mother' who had been kidnapped therefrom."

Emerson was impressed with the superiority of the manners of Charlestonians white and black, but the most memorable event of his winter in the South was his meeting with Prince Achille Murat, a nephew of Napoleon, now married to an American and living on a plantation near Tallahassee. When Emerson sailed for Charleston, Murat went with him, and they talked incessantly. In Murat, Emerson found what he had not believed to exist: "a consistent atheist" and as ardent a lover of the truth as himself. Murat must have done something to shake some of the young minister's provincial notions, but Emerson presumably saw in Murat not a highly intelligent Southern planter but a European intellectual.

For eight years after his return from the South one finds in Emerson's writings few comments on the South or slavery. His conscience apparently did not deeply trouble him about slavery until the antislavery controversy became acute. As time went on, men who owed much of their culture to slaveholding Rome, Greece, and

Palestine began to denounce Southern slaveholders as representatives of a semibarbarous civilization. Then the serene and philosophic Emerson was swept along by the tide exactly like lesser men. In the New England of his day, however, no one would remind him that in "The American Scholar" he had said: "Is it not the chief disgrace in the world, not to be an unit . . . but to be reckoned in the gross, in the hundred, or the thousand, of the party, the section, to which we belong; and our opinion predicted geographically, as the north, or the south?"

By October, 1837, Emerson had come to view the Southern collegian much more critically. The young Southerner who came to Cambridge was "a spoiled child," "a mere parader," "a mere bladder of conceit." "Each snipper-snapper of them all undertakes to speak for the entire Southern States." They were, however, he admitted, "more civilized than the Seminoles . . . a little more."

In 1846, when he wrote the memorable "Ode Inscribed to W. H. Channing," Emerson was still not willing to take to the abolitionist platform, and he was not, like some of the extremists, willing to break up the Union. He wrote:

> What boots thy zeal,
> O glowing friend,
> That would indignant rend
> The northland from the south?
> Wherefore? to what good end?
> Boston Bay and Bunker Hill
> Would serve things still. . . .

The crisis of 1850 moved Emerson to begin calculating the value of the Union—something which Thomas Cooper had advised South Carolinians to do some twenty years earlier. The new and more stringent fugitive slave law moved him to write in the *Journals:* "This filthy enactment was made in the nineteenth century, by people who could read and write. I will not obey it, by God." Speaking in Concord in 1851, he said: "Under the Union

I suppose the fact to be that there are really two nations, the North and the South." Some Southerners would thus far have agreed with him but probably not in keeping to the conclusion that "The Union is at an end as soon as an immoral law is enacted." Until the war came, Emerson was willing that the masters should at enormous cost to the nation be compensated for the loss of their property in slaves; but when he read his "Boston Hymn" on January 1, 1863, he said:

> Pay ransom to the owner
> And fill the bag to the brim.
> Who is the owner? The slave is owner
> And ever was. Pay him.

On May 19, 1856, Emerson's friend Charles Sumner delivered in the United States Senate a vitriolic tirade entitled "The Crime against Kansas," in which he shamefully abused Senator Andrew P. Butler of South Carolina. Butler's young kinsman Preston S. Brooks, a member of the House of Representatives, retaliated by striking Sumner to the floor with his cane. Many but by no means all Southerners defended Brooks, but in New England Sumner was regarded as a martyr. Emerson said in a Concord address:

I do not see how a barbarous community and a civilized community can constitute one state. I think we must get rid of slavery, or we must get rid of freedom. Life has not parity of value in the free state and in the slave state. In one, it is adorned with education, with skilful labor, with arts, with long prospective interests, with sacred family ties, with honor and justice. In the other, life is a fever; man is an animal, given to pleasure, frivolous, irritable, spending his days in hunting and practising with deadly weapons to defend himself against his slaves and against his companions brought up in the same idle and dangerous way. Such people live for the moment, they have properly no future, and readily risk on every passion a life which is of small value to themselves or to others.

Emerson had come to accept the abolitionist legend of a barbarous South. He had forgotten his friend Barnwell when he added: "The whole state of South Carolina does not now offer one or any number of persons who are to be weighed in the scale with such a person as the meanest of them all has now struck down." This is even more ungenerous than a passage in a letter written by William Gilmore Simms on the last day of 1860: "Charleston is worth all New England."

In November, 1859, Emerson referred to John Brown, then under sentence of death, as "that new saint, than whom none purer or more brave was ever led by love of men into conflict and death, —the new saint awaiting his martyrdom, and who, if he shall suffer, will make the gallows glorious like the cross." A truer estimate of Brown is found in a passage that Hawthorne, no lover of reformers, wrote with Emerson in mind: ". . . nor did I expect ever to shrink so unutterably from any apothegm of a sage, whose happy lips have uttered a hundred golden sentences, as that saying . . . that the death of this bloodstained fanatic has 'made the Gallows as venerable as the Cross!' Nobody was ever more justly hanged."

While the Southern states were seceding one by one, Emerson took the same position as Hawthorne and Whittier that the North was well rid of them and no compromise should be made to bring them back. The attack on Fort Sumter, however, affected Emerson and millions of other Northerners as the Japanese attack on Pearl Harbor affected a later generation. Now the secessionists must be punished and the Southern states forcibly brought back into a Union which they hated.

This brief survey needs to be somewhat qualified. Except in the case of Preston S. Brooks, Emerson did not denounce individual Southerners. He always gave the Southerners credit for courage. Two years after the war he could say: "Of course, there are noble men everywhere, and there are such in the South. . . ." He had to add, however: "But the common people, rich and poor, were the narrowest and most conceited of mankind, as arrogant as the negroes on the Gambia River; and, by the way, it looks as if the editors of the Southern press were in all times selected from this class." Emerson would have been surprised if someone had told him how large a number of these Southern editors were natives of New England.

The rest of the story shows Emerson and the South in a more pleasant light. On July 6, 1866, he wrote to his old friend Barnwell, urging him to attend a reunion of the class of 1821: "But I wish you to know that distance, politics, war, even, at last, have not been able to efface in any manner the high affectionate regard in which I, in common I believe with all your old contemporaries of 1817–21, have firmly held you as our avowed chief, in days when boys, as we then were, give a tender & romantic value to that distinction, which they cannot later give again."

In the spring of 1876 the two literary societies of the University of Virginia asked Emerson to deliver an address in Charlottesville as a part of the commencement program. Emerson, now seventy-three years old, had given up speaking in public; but he accepted the invitation, "thinking it of happy omen that they should send to Massachusetts for their orator." "The visitors," Emerson and his daughter, says J. E. Cabot, "were treated with every attention in the society of the place, there was no intentional discourtesy, but the Southern self-respect appeared to demand that they should be constantly reminded that they were in an oppressed and abused country. And the next day, at Emerson's address, the audience in general—mostly young women with their admirers, but also children, as well as older persons—seemed to regard the occasion chiefly as one for social entertainment, and there was so much noise that he could not make himself heard." Emerson probably could not at that time have made himself heard by the entire audience if there had been perfect quiet. Finding themselves unable to hear, the youngsters talked, as others were to do six years later when a Southern writer, George W. Cable, was delivering a commencement address at the University of Mississippi. Emerson's friends were somewhat indignant; but when Cabot asked him about his reception in Virginia, all he would say was: "They are very brave people down there, and say just what they think."

In Charlottesville Emerson met several persons who had read his books and expressed their pleasure in meeting him. The next day in the train for the North many of his fellow-travelers, on their way to the Philadelphia Exposition, asked to be introduced to him. Reconstruction was coming to an end, and the South, which had not been hospitable to many New England writers, was at last coming to accept Emerson as a contemporary classic. It had taken a long time, for it was difficult for any Southerner to understand the Unitarian-transcendentalist background out of which Emerson's writings had grown. By 1877, however, Sidney Lanier, who had grown up in a Presbyterian home in Macon, Georgia, was writing to Bayard Taylor that he would like to discuss with him "Emerson, whom I have been reading all winter, and who gives me immeasurable delight because he does not propound to me disagreeable systems and hideous creeds but simply walks along high and bright ways where one loves to go with him—then I am ready to praise God for the circumstance that if corn were a dollar a bushel I could not with my present finances buy a lunch for a pony."

Emerson's writings, which were often misunderstood even in his native Massachusetts, held peculiar difficulties for Southern readers in the forties and fifties. One exasperated Southern reviewer wrote: ". . . Mr. Emerson writes in a language which even his own children cannot understand." Even yet Emerson's poetic, oracular, semiclerical language sometimes misleads the unwary reader. Then, too, Emerson had . . . his provincial side; and the Southern reader, who had his own provincialisms, was often repelled. Lowell thought Emerson the most American of our writers; few Southerners would have agreed with him. A not untypical reaction was that of Joel R. Poinsett, one of the ablest

and most intelligent Southerners of his time. The Swedish novelist
Fredrika Bremer records her experience with Poinsett in the
late forties:

I wished to make him a little acquainted with my friends the transcendentalists and idealists of the North, and I have read to him por-
tions of Emerson's *Essays*. But they shoot over the head of the old
statesman; he says it is all "unpractical," and he often criticizes it un-
justly, and we quarrel. . . . Mr. Poinsett is, nevertheless, struck with
Emerson's brilliant aphorisms, and says that he will buy his works.
It is remarkable how very little, or not at all, the authors of the Northern states, even the best of them, are known in the South. They are
afraid of admitting their liberal opinions into the slave states.

For orthodox Southerners Emerson was an exponent of heretical
doctrines that were dangerous. By this time the Southern churches
had broken with the Northern, which they regarded as tainted with
rationalism and fanatical on the slavery question. In January,
1852, John Custis Darby of Lexington, Kentucky, published an
article on "Ralph Waldo Emerson" in the *Quarterly Review* of the
Southern branch of the Methodist Church. "Mr. Emerson," he
said, "is the representative of the New England infidelity; at the
head of which form of doctrines, stands Strauss of Germany."
For Emerson, as for Strauss, he thought, biblical history had only
a symbolic value. "Strauss receives the truth, but denies the record
as genuine, authentic history. . . . There is no God; it is all a
myth." "It is a favorite doctrine with him [Emerson] to praise
and admire the doctrines and excellencies of all religions except
Christianity; and if he name the latter, to disparage it by a comparison with the doctrines of Vishnu and the philosophy of Plato.
Among his representative men, the only Christian he has chosen to
introduce, is the good and the learned, but the deranged Swedenborg."
A curious example of the Southern religious objection to Emerson is found in the second novel of Augusta Jane Evans, *Beulah*

(1859). Its popularity suggests that in other sections there were many readers who regarded Emerson as an infidel. Beulah, a studious orphan girl, "with a slowly dying faith," is reading books one would not expect a Southern girl to read—although Miss Evans herself had evidently read them.

It was no longer study for the sake of erudition; these riddles involved all that she prized in Time and Eternity, and she grasped books of every description with the eagerness of a famishing nature. What dire chance threw into her hands such works as Emerson's, Carlyle's, and Goethe's? Like the waves of the clear, sunny sea, they only increased her thirst to madness. Her burning lips were ever at these fountains; and, in her reckless eagerness, she plunged into the gulf of German speculation.

Somewhat later Beulah has a long conversation with her friend Cornelia Graham, a widely traveled young woman who is rapidly becoming an invalid. Cornelia has absorbed the "grim Emersonian fatalism" completely, but Beulah has come to the conclusion that "of all Pyrrhonists he is the prince."

Beulah took up one of the volumes, and turned the pages carelessly.
    "But all this would shock a Christian."
    "And deservedly; for Emerson's works, collectively and individually, are aimed at the doctrines of Christianity. There is a grim, terrible fatalism scowling on his pages which might well frighten the reader who clasped the Bible to his heart."
    "Yet you accept his 'compensation.' Are you prepared to receive his deistic system?" Cornelia leaned forward and spoke eagerly. Beulah smiled.
    "Why strive to cloak the truth? I should not term his fragmentary system 'deistic.' He knows not yet what he believes. There are singular antagonisms existing among even his pet theories."

When Cornelia replies, "I have not found any," Beulah points them out and adds: "His writings are, to me, like heaps of broken glass, beautiful in the individual crystal, sparkling, and often dazzling, but gather them up, and try to fit them into a whole, and the jagged edges refuse to unite."

Cornelia on her deathbed says: "Oh, the so-called philosophers of this century and the last are crowned-heads of humbugry [*sic*]! . . . They mock earnest, inquiring minds with their refined infinitesimal, homeopathic 'developments' of deity; metaphysical wolves in Socratic cloaks. Oh, they have much to answer for!" She admits that she has finally lost faith in Emerson and Theodore Parker: "Emerson's atheistic fatalism is enough to unhinge human reason; he is a great, and I believe an honest thinker, and of his genius I have the profoundest admiration. An intellectual Titan, he wages war with received creeds, and rising on the ruins of systems, struggles to scale the battlements of truth. As for Parker, a careful perusal of his works was enough to disgust me." In the end Cornelia dies without recovering her faith. Beulah is more fortunate, for her faith returns and so does her lover, who had vanished somewhere in China.

The fairest and ablest discussion of Emerson that I have found in the ante-bellum Southern magazines is Daniel K. Whitaker's "Transcendentalism," published in the *Southern Quarterly Review* in October, 1842. It is a review of the first two volumes of *The Dial*. Whitaker had grown up in Massachusetts and, though he did not like it, he had some understanding of what transcendentalism was. "The transcendentalists," he wrote, "are the enemies of antiquity, and equally hostile to existing institutions, and prevaling [*sic*] systems in morals, in philosophy, and religion. They are the champions of change and reform in all things." Thus they endangered the entire social and economic order. The transcendentalists had no philosophic system and were, as Whitaker perceived, united only "by sympathy of spirit." Their heresies were only "opinions that were prevalent previous to the time of Locke, and which appear to us to have been fully met, and triumphantly re-

futed, by that illustrious metaphysician." Whitaker indulged in no
denunciation, but he mildly ridiculed a passage in one of Emerson's essays.

William Gilmore Simms was greatly irritated by Lowell's *A
Fable for Critics,* which omitted all Southern writers except Poe.
"This critic, for example," he wrote in the *Southern Quarterly
Review* for October, 1849, "expends all his praise upon the chil-
dren of the East. He finds no others in the country, or, if he does,
he dismisses them with a scornful complacency. . . ."

Hear our satirist discourse on Emerson, whom he styles a "Greek
head on Yankee shoulders," and you fancy him one of the most marvelous men that the world has produced. A parallel is run between him
and Carlyle, greatly to the discredit of the latter. None less than Plato
will content him for a comparison. . . . And all this said of a man who
is really half-witted, and whose chief excellence consists in mystifying
the simple and disguising commonplaces in allegory. One Mr. Alcott
follows, of whom we know nothing. . . .

In July, 1850, writing in the same periodical nine months later,
Simms wrote in a calmer mood:

Emerson is an able essayist, of a school too much on stilts, too ambitious of the mystical, to be always secure of the sensible and true. He
is decidedly popular with the "transcendentalists," if we may recognize,
by a term so dignified, a rather inflated race, who presume somewhat
upon the fact that their place of birth is a few degrees nearer the rising
sun than ours. Emerson aims to be a reformer, after the fashion of
Carlyle; and no doubt has large merits, which might be available to
common and beneficial use if they were less clouded and embarrassed
with his affectations of the Delphic.

One of the fairest reviews is found in *De Bow's* review of *The
Conduct of Life* in March, 1861, the month of Lincoln's inaugura-
tion:

Under this title, Ticknor & Fields publish in their usual attractive
style, the most recent volume of the writings of Ralph Waldo Emerson. We do not profess to be among the admirers of that eccentric

gentleman, either as a man or as an author, but we do not deny that he possesses talent of a high order, possibly it might not be improper to say, genius. In not only this last, but in all of his works, we find many striking and original thoughts, but they are generally clothed in a style affectedly, studiously, and elaborately involved and obscure. They are not "apples of gold set in pictures of silver," but rather like pearls embedded in a mudhole, which it requires much patient industry to find. The followers of Mr. Emerson, and we believe that their name is not legion in these latitudes, will find in "The Conduct of Life," the usual characteristics of their favorite.

Long after 1861 intelligent Southerners found a difficulty in appreciating Emerson. Even Paul Hamilton Hayne, who had met Emerson and was an admirer of his *English Traits* and some of his poems, wished, as he wrote to Mrs. Julia C. R. Dorr, May 16, 1882, "that his *Essays* were *some* of them *clearer,* and informed by a loftier spirit of Faith; instead of that vague species of half-Pantheistic philosophy, which after all, is pre-eminently unoriginal, a mere *elaborated echo* of the 'Neo-Platonism' of Alexandria in the fourth and fifth centuries." On April 15, 1895, Joel Chandler Harris wrote in reply to William Malone Baskervill's inquiry about his favorite authors that the book which had first attracted his attention and held it longest was *The Vicar of Wakefield:*

Apart from this, all good books have me interested more or less. But the queer self-consciousness of Emerson has never appealed to me as strongly as it has to some of my friends. This is not Emerson's fault, but mine. You cannot expect an uncultured Georgia cracker to follow patiently the convolute diagrams of the Over-Soul. I find Sir Thomas Browne far more stimulating (I hope I am not treading on your corns here. Confidentially, Emerson's attitude as the New England Bigod— if I may use so crude an expression—has amused me no little). You see I am perfectly frank in this, presenting the appearance of feeling as proud of my lack of taste and culture as a little girl is of her rag doll. It may give you a cue.

Simms and Whitaker were not ashamed to admit a failure to see in Emerson a great writer; Harris was. By 1895 Southerners had come somewhat reluctantly to accept, as a part of the new order, the Northern rating of Emerson and other New England writers.

That was well enough, but one Southern scholar at least was disturbed because, as it seemed to him, Southerners were accepting also the low Northern estimate of the writers of the Old South. In 1899 Professor Charles W. Kent, of the University of Virginia, said in a commencement address at the University of Tennessee: "I venture the assertion that our Southern youth today are as familiar with the writers of the New England school as are the boys of Boston or of Concord, but the New England boys—alas! it is true of our Southern youth as well—are lamentably ignorant of the literature of the South."

DANIEL AARON

✪

Emerson as Democrat

As Tocqueville says, democracy makes "every man forget his ancestors" (a desirable end from Hawthorne's and Melville's point of view, although both are fascinated by the past) and democracy "separates his contemporaries from him; it throws him back forever upon himself alone, and threatens in the end to confine him entirely within the solitude of his own heart." Here, if you will, is the Unpardonable Sin, or, to put it still another way, the great transcendental fallacy, which emerges most clearly in the writings of Emerson.

Emerson's simultaneous acceptance and rejection of American civilization illustrates the condition of the divided intelligence even

One of the main marks of Emerson's character was a polarity which he sometimes softened into ambivalence. At its simplest and clearest, he saw a sharp opposition in himself, the opposition for example between matter and spirit; yet at times he also believed that one could complement the other. At its most complex, he wavered back and forth between delicately balanced opposites. The able social historian Daniel Aaron looks at the relationship of Emerson's ambivalence to the progressive tradition. In doing so, sometimes a bit rigorously, he shows us Emerson's character in its all too human aspects. His Emerson looks illogical, inconsistent; he is both pro-democratic and anti-democratic, both critical of material success and impressed by it. The selection given here, untitled in the book, is from *Men of Good Hope* by Professor Aaron. Copyright 1951 by Oxford University Press, Inc. Reprinted by permission.

more strikingly than the ambivalent positions of Hawthorne and Melville. He was both the critic and the celebrator of his and subsequent generations, the Yea-sayer and the Nay-sayer. By Tocqueville's standards he was the most articulate exponent of democratic individualism, whose philosophy of self-reliance, or self-sufficiency, harmonized with the disintegrative tendencies of American life, and yet at the same time he quite characteristically attacked the social consequences of his own philosophy.

This contradiction also appears, although to a lesser extent, in the ideas of the reformers who regarded themselves as his disciples or who unconsciously reflected his influence; and since Emerson was the real prophet of the progressive tradition—the Scholar without plan or system, who impressed men of all radical creeds— his polarized attitude toward the individual has a direct bearing on the history of progressivism in America. For the progressives who followed him felt his impatience with men in the mass—this "maudlin agglutination," as Emerson put it. Like him, they held forth the possibility of human development while noting the appalling evidences of human mediocrity. Like him again, they fervently condemned the shortsightedness and selfishness of the middle class at the same time that they cherished its virtues and faith. Emerson was their perfect representative, and his ambivalent attitude toward man in the aggregate was shared by the progressives who followed him.

Consider first his lesser role as the seer of *laisser-faire* capitalism and the rampant individual.

To anyone who has habitually imagined Emerson as the sedentary philosopher invariably upholding with transcendental logic the Ideal-Real against the evanescent Material, his delight in the harmonies of the market place might appear somewhat paradoxical. A closer survey of his writings, however, shows that his communications with the Over-Soul did not always preclude a secular interest in vulgar appearances. His transcendentalism, in fact, provided an ideal explanation for the conduct and activities of the business classes and offered the necessary criteria by which he was able to justify or to criticize them. This leisure-loving beneficiary of a commercial economy, whose antecedents were ministerial rather than mercantile, outlined a rationale for the entrepreneur of an industrial age.

Emerson's fastidious tastes found little that was congenial in the vulgarity and crassness of workaday business. It is all the more remarkable that he was able to sublimate his instinctive distaste for the hucksters in counting-houses and see them finally as exemplifying divine principles. His *Journals* and *Essays* are filled with disparaging references to the business classes; their sordidness, their undeviating pursuit of wealth, their narrow self-interests, and their timidity are bluntly and scornfully arraigned. But he seems to have cherished a particular dislike only for the meaner of the species. Businessmen of larger appetites and bolder ambitions, notwithstanding their faults, often called forth his admiration, and he consistently identified business intrepidity with the exploits of warriors and heroes.

The portrait of Napoleon in *Representative Men* is perhaps the best illustration of Emerson's ambivalent attitude toward aggressiveness and self-seeking; it is not by accident that he saw "this deputy of the nineteenth century" as the "agent or attorney of the middle class of modern society; of the throng who fill the markets, shops, counting-houses, manufactories, ships, of the modern world, aiming to be rich." The essay falls roughly into two parts. In the first section Emerson exalts Napoleon into a superman; in the concluding three or four paragraphs, he dwells fiercely upon his uglier defects—his coarseness and lack of ideality. "In short," Emerson concludes, "when you have penetrated through all the circles of power and splendor, you were not dealing with a gentleman, at last; but with an imposter and a rogue."

But the deflation of the great man undertaken at the close of the essay cannot entirely obliterate the earlier impression of Emerson's enthusiastic admiration, which he shared with thousands of his American contemporaries. In praising Napoleon's practicality, prudence, and directness, his powers of synthesis and cool audacity, Emerson is underscoring precisely those attributes that made up the American success code; his emphasis helps to explain the peculiar fascination Napoleon held for the warriors of American business. Emerson's strictures against the blowhard, the strutting egotist, the low vulgarian are devastating, but the following encomium also represents his settled convictions:

> We cannot, in the universal imbecility, indecision and indolence of men, sufficiently congratulate ourselves on this strong and ready actor, who took occasion by the beard, and showed us how much may be accomplished by the mere force of such virtues as all men possess in less degrees; namely, by punctuality, by personal attention, by courage, and thoroughness.

Emerson's respect for power and its achievements is even more glowingly expressed in two other essays, "Power" and "Wealth." Here he reiterates his preference for the "bruisers" and "pirates," the "men of the right Caesarian pattern" who transcend the pettiness of "talkers" and "clerks" and dominate the world by sheer force of character. "Life is a search after power," he announces, and the successful men who understand the laws of Nature and respond to the Godhead within themselves, who convert "the sap and juices of the planet to the incarnation and nutriment of their design," are unconsciously fulfilling the plan of a benevolent Providence.

In these essays and elsewhere, Emerson was not only synchronizing the predatory practices of the entrepreneur with the harmony of the universe and permitting merchants (as Bronson Alcott shrewdly said) to "find a refuge from their own duplicity under his broad shield"; he was also outlining a code of behavior that the superior man must follow, and sketching the ideal political economy under which the superman might best exercise his uncommon talents. Specialize, he advised, "elect your work" and "drop all the rest." Do not dissipate your efforts. Concentrate! "Concentration is the secret of strength in politics, in war, in trade, in short all management of human affairs." Make up your mind and stick to your decisions. Practice again and again; it is constant drilling that distinguishes the professional from the amateur and enables the "indifferent hacks and mediocrities" to win out over men of superior abilities. He quoted the business slogans of Poor Richard with warm approval and identified "counting-room maxims" with the "laws of the universe."

Emerson's optimistic faith, his belief that all apparent evil ultimately cancels out into good, allowed him to view the depredations of business more tranquilly than, let us say, a Theodore Parker, less given to transcendentalizing business enterprise. A little wickedness, Emerson believed, served as a kind of energizing principle. "Men of this surcharge of arterial blood cannot live on nuts, herb-tea, and elegies," he characteristically remarked. The hot speculators exploiting the country, the "monomaniacs" of trade who clash in the market place, build up the country as they enrich themselves. Unworldly moralists who rant against the violence of competition are in reality working against the laws of the world. Were they successful in their efforts to subdue the spirit of competitive enterprise, they would be forced to rekindle the fires of avarice if civilization were to continue. Thus it inevitably followed that any attempt to check the capitalistic incentives was a futile and unjustifiable interference with the iron laws of circumstance:

Wealth brings with it its own checks and balances. The basis of political economy is non-interference. The only safe role is found in the self-adjusting meter of demand and supply. Do not legislate. Meddle, and you snap the sinews with your sumptuary laws. Give no bounties, make equal laws, secure life and property, and you need not give alms. Open the doors of opportunity to talent and virtue and they will do themselves justice, and property will not be in bad hands. In a free and just commonwealth, property rushes from the idle and imbecile to the industrious, brave and persevering.

Quotations like this represent only a single strain in Emerson's thought. Equally eloquent passages might be included in which he affirms his strong democratic attachments and humanitarian sympathies, but the Nietzschean side of Emerson is unmistakable. As a transcendentalist he had to recognize the divine potentialities of all men and to reconcile all social manifestations with the general will of God. Hence his interest in and sympathy with all causes and movements, however absurd, and his tolerance of creeds and men not instinctively congenial to him. His conservative and autocratic biases, however, reasserted themselves from time to time, just as the materiality he philosophically denied anchored his rhapsodic speculations to brute fact. Emerson enjoyed almost sensuously the plump and solid tangibles, and he admired the "inventive or creative class" that made them possible.

Running through his writings is a constant disparagement of men in the mass, the "imbeciles," as he calls them on several occasions, the "uninventive or accepting class" held down by "gravity, custom, and fear" and tyrannized by convention. What quickened his faith in the latent capacities of man was the "grand" talent rising like a huge wave over the placid ocean of humanity. Although Emerson lived in rural Concord during periods of economic and political upheaval, he sanctioned unconsciously the forces of exploitation that were at work in the United States and the powerful men, impelled by what he called a "keener avarice," who were directing this exploitation. Rarely does he credit the collective energies of the common man as the great transforming power. Man in the mass is inert until galvanized by the great captains of enterprise. Wealth is created by ability, and it is the rich man "who can avail himself of all man's faculties . . . The world is his tool-chest, and he is successful, or his education is carried on just so far, as is the marriage of his faculties with nature, or the degree in which he takes up things into himself."

It would not be too extreme to say that Emerson envisaged the scholar as employing these "business principles" in exploiting the frontiers of the mind, drawing "a benefit from the labors of the greatest number of men, of men in distant countries and in past times." The function of Emerson's scholar was to mold the plastic world and shake the "cowed" and the "trustless" out of their lethargy. The scholar was to create an intellectual revolution by gradually "domesticating" the idea of culture (the metaphor is Emerson's) and to illustrate the proved maxim that "he who has put forth his total strength in fit actions has the richest return of wisdom." After a period of worry and doubts, the Emerson who agonized over the choice of his vocation was able to reconcile the divergent appeals of practical action and reflection in the vocation of the scholar, which became for him a symbol of dynamic passivity.

Whether or not there is any truth in the contention expressed above, it can be plausibly argued that Emerson's "transcendentalizing" of business conduct testified to his awareness of the growing significance of commerce and industry in American life. When an age is dominated by the economic mind, Henry Adams once observed, "the imaginative mind tends to adopt its form and its faults." By temperament, inclination, and circumstance, Emerson belonged to a class out of sympathy with the rising industrial *bourgeoisie,* but he was extremely sensitive to the currents of his age and deeply infected by its omnipresent materialism. Ostensibly preoccupied with nonutilitarian ends, he nevertheless showed an almost inordinate interest in the practical performances of men and their mundane accomplishments.

Emerson helps us to see the motive forces that drove American individualists to absorb themselves in money-making; he makes

clear their ambition and self-reliance, their inspired faith in limitless opportunities. His emphasis on the value of natural exploitation, of opening the world like an oyster, was only a more articulate and rhetorical expression of what millions already dimly felt,
and his celebration of the practical doers was a kind of transcendental concession to those who scorned the useless visionary. He
had been impressed by the magnificence of American commercial
and industrial enterprise, by the dramatic implications of a continent unsubdued. To a romantic and poetic nature, such a phenomenon helped to compensate for the drabness and sameness of
American life, to reduce the tedium of democratic anonymity. It
allowed him to celebrate audacious individual accomplishment,
and it gave a martial air to a nation of civilian traders. "Whatever
appeals to the imagination, by transcending the ordinary limits of
human nobility," Emerson said in speaking of Napoleon, "wonderfully encourages and liberates us." Emerson encouraged his countrymen to cultivate their inward greatness, and one of the ways
he did so was to glorify the characters and deeds of the world's
heroes who followed transcendental impulses.

Neither Emerson nor his disciples, oddly enough, saw any connection between the cult of self-trust and the mercenary paradise
about to be revealed after 1865, although a closer perusal of
Tocqueville might have hinted as much. Emerson was simply
acknowledging, perhaps unduly, a side of the national character
that was aggressive and rapacious, that hated physical impediments, whether things or people. The significance of the frontier
has been exaggerated, but the fact that for two centuries it represented a challenge and an obstacle as well as an opportunity to
generations of "go-getters" is of crucial importance in understanding the American experience. If the frontier did not make the
American character, it whetted the appetites and aggravated the
assertive compulsions of the men who camped along its fringes.

Another kind of individualism, however, that took root and flourished in America did not express itself in a compulsion to dominate, to impose by force. Rather it emphasized the need for individual fulfillment and enlargement, for self-containment and passive growth. Individualism, taken in this sense, did not manifest itself in gouging the outer world, in fighting and scrambling in order to keep one's identity. It encouraged inner cultivation, and insofar as it was concerned with external realities—the problems of government and economics and culture—it conceived of them in terms of individual welfare. This kind of individualism or Personalism regarded the "self" as a rare and tender thing. Thoreau caught its spirit when he wrote: "The finest qualities of our nature, like the bloom on fruits, can be preserved only by the most delicate handling." And Emerson reflected this passive and humane conception of individualism even more unmistakably than he did its aggressive antitype. If as a Yankee he sympathized with the latter and vicariously enjoyed the corps of the unshrinking entrepreneurs, as a Poet and Seer he repudiated them and their philosophy.

Emerson, a radical wedded to principle, never intended his exhortations to justify the practices of "robber barons." In fact Emerson came to have a supreme contempt for the commercial mentality. He made fun of State Street timidity. He charged the bankers with fearing transcendentalism, because it would unsettle property and impair the obligation of contract. The businessman, he said, preferred slavery to illegality. Emerson addressed himself, finally, to democrats and humanitarians, not to property-worshipers, and for every conservative who hailed him there were a dozen reformers who constructed their systems upon his radical assumptions.

Emerson's political philosophy—it might be called transcendental democracy—had marked Jeffersonian and Jacksonian overtones. Strongly individualistic, it also spoke for equality of opportunity in economic and political affairs, and it lent support to the belief in *laisser faire* and the necessity of the minimized state. But it was more spiritual and intellectual than the organized movements for political democracy and less concerned with political and economic considerations, less a matter of economic rationalization. Its chief proponents tended to be professional and literary people; ministers, writers, teachers, and reformers made up its ranks rather than businessmen, officeholders, or lawyers. This is not to say that the transcendentalists played down political and economic questions—far from it—but they were not defenders of an "interest" or a "faction." If they had no desire to capture and operate a government, they stubbornly protested when government overstepped its limited confines and by its acts trespassed on their spiritual domain.

The men and women who made up this transcendental corps were mostly of New England origin, although a handful were born outside New England. As children of the professional or commercial classes or of the sturdy farming yeomanry, they received educational advantages above the average of their day, and for the most part they came from families distinguished neither by great wealth nor by poverty. Almost all of them seemed to have been reared in homes where the business of life was taken seriously and idealistically. It was this group that, disgusted by the prevailing materialism of the day, turned to culture and to reform.

Although the reformers shared their contemporaries' faith in progress, they could not accept the corollary that America was the best of all possible worlds or that the American experiment could be called a complete success. Shocked by the materialism and the inhumanity they saw everywhere about them, they found themselves in the position of condemning the social practices and behavior of a class with whom they were closely connected by birth and education and of speaking for an underprivileged group with whom they had little in common. Like the intelligentsia in societies before and after, they deliberately alienated themselves from the moneyed interests who had nurtured and sustained them. Because they still took seriously the Puritan tradition of stewardship, of class obligations, at a time when community responsibilities were being increasingly ignored, they could not be oblivious to the ruinous consequences of "enlightened self-interest." Many of them, moreover, believed quite literally in natural rights and other eighteenth-century humanitarian doctrines that proclaimed the necessity of the mutual concern of every man for another. Since the transcendentalists respected the sacredness of the human individuality, the crassness and the insensitivity of the employing classes, indeed most of the values of the rising business elite, were personally distasteful to them.

Although Emerson was the most famous exponent of the transcendentalized democratic philosophy, his was neither the most original nor the most incisive mind among the New England reformers. William Ellery Channing had prepared the way for him; Thoreau and Whitman developed certain strains of his thought more acutely and profoundly; and Theodore Parker, as we shall see, surpassed him as a political and economic analyst. But Emerson, the master transcendentalist, somehow subsumed them all and most successfully comprehended his age. In him, as Howells wrote, "conscience and intellect were angelically one."

Emerson's political ideas emerged quite logically from transcendental principles. He believed in a divine power sometimes referred to as the Over-Soul, and he taught that all men shared in that divinity or at least were capable of establishing a rapport with it. Men's joint participation in this Spirit, their common share of the divine inheritance, made them brothers and gave the lie to artificial distinctions. In the great democracy of spirit that Emerson conjured up as a kind of Platonic archetype of the imperfect American model, all men were potentially great. Men were not great in fact (Emerson had no such leveling ideas, as we have seen), but

every man could be great if he harkened to the admonition of the
Over-Soul in himself.

Like John Adams and Thomas Jefferson, Emerson believed in
a natural aristocracy, although his *aristoi* bore little resemblance
to Jefferson's. Society divided itself into the men of understanding
and the men of Reason. The former, the most numerous and the
most ordinary, lived in "a world of pig-lead" and acted as if
"rooted and grounded in adamant." Sunk in this profound materialism, they lacked the imaginative penetration of the true aristocrats, the men of Reason, who plumbed the spiritual reality
behind the world of fact. The men of Reason—poets, seers, philos-
opers, scholars—the passive doers, served humanity as the geogra-
phers of the "supersensible regions" and inspired "an audacious
mental outlook." They formed no inflexible caste, but they wonderfully "liberated" the cramped average afraid to trust itself.

Emerson did not intend his political theories to provide a sanc-
tion for social lawlessness, even though his celebration of the individual intuition, abstracted from the body of his thinking, seemed
to justify an aggressive individualism. If it encouraged the predatory entrepreneur, it also invalidated contracts. It dissolved the
power of tyrannical authority; it undermined tradition. If carried
to its logical conclusion, the Emersonian theory that every person
should act as a majority of one would result in anarchism, but
he never pushed this idea to its end. Although his writings are filled
with disparaging remarks about the state as the "principal obstruction and nuisance with which we have to contend," he opposed it
only when it sought to supervene the higher laws, when it prevented men from living naturally and wisely and justly.

His views on the function of government were by no means entirely negative. Government, he said, "was set up for the protection
and comfort of all good citizens." If the withered state represented
his ultimate ideal, he could subscribe to Thoreau's remark: "To
speak practically . . . I ask for, not at once no government, but

at once a better government." He explained the community experiment at Brook Farm as proceeding

in great part from a feeling that the true offices of the state, the state
has let fall to the ground; that in the scramble of parties for the public
purse, the main duties of government were omitted,—the duty to in-
struct the ignorant, to supply the poor with work, and . . . the medi-
ation between want and supply.

Emerson reached this mature and liberal view of government
and its purpose after a considerable amount of candid self-exami-
nation and after a long look at his own country. But Emerson came
to believe that the Democrats had the best principles if not the
best men, and the more he dirtied himself with politics (for he
regarded the demands of the social world with resentment and
anger) the more disgusted he became with the "thin and watery
blood of Whiggism."

Instead of having its own aims passionately in view, it cants about
the policy of a Washington and a Jefferson. It speaks to expectation
and not the torrent of its wishes and needs, waits for its antagonist to
speak that it may have something to oppose, and, failing that, having
nothing to say, is happy to hurrah.

Emerson's contempt for timid conservatism is best conveyed in his
sarcastic description of its doctrine: "Better endure tyranny according to law a thousand years than irregular unconstitutional
happiness for a day."

That he could feel this way about a conservatism continuously on
the defensive and still retain his affection and respect for the "active, intelligent, well-meaning and wealthy part of the people"
who made up its party is characteristic not only of Emerson but
also of the middle-class reformers who succeeded him. Like Emerson, they belonged to that corps of sensitive intellectuals who
placed spiritual values above material ones and human considera-

tions above the rights of property. Like him, they made the flowering of the individual personality their ultimate goal and estimated all political and social ideologies, whether conservative or radical, by this single test. They had no quarrel with the machine nor did they advocate a return to a smokeless, factoryless America. They repudiated Thoreau's remedy by isolation, for they agreed completely with Mazzini's repeated injunction that the only way an individual man could fuse with his fellows was through social institutions. Although desiring a more equitable distribution of the wealth produced by the new technology, they did not stop with material consideration. To preserve the integrity of "souls" suffocating in the impersonal fog of the market system, to eliminate the evils so inextricably bound up with industrialism, these seemed to them the most pressing responsibilities of the reformer. . . .

H. L. KLEINFIELD

✪

The Structure of Emerson's Death

Emerson died at a serene age a serene death, befitting his contemplative life. At seventy-nine he already showed signs of mental weakness, a failing memory, and fitful coherency, before a fever separated him altogether from intelligible discourses. On the day he died, his mind cleared almost proverbially at noon, then lapsed into an unbroken coma until he exhaled his last breath early in the evening of April 27, 1882. In the house of his ancestors he was folded to their bosoms while surrounded by his family and close friends, who for days had been hoping against the known outcome.

The public mourned Emerson with both grief and joy. Editorial opinion composed a chorus in which some voices sounded greater

How Emerson looked to America at the end of his career is described in this essay by the cultural historian H. L. Kleinfield. Emerson's death impelled the journalists and literary journeymen of his time to some of their gaudiest rhetoric. They obviously felt that a great man deserved a great effort. They strained to do him justice and, as Professor Kleinfield's lavish quotations show, they almost never succeeded. Notwithstanding, they leave us with a sense of what Emerson meant to his countrymen and, thanks to Professor Kleinfield's work, an appreciation of the psychology behind their rhetorical response. The essay appeared in the *Bulletin of the New York Public Library*, LXV (January 1961), 47–64. It is reprinted here, slightly revised and abridged by the author, with his permission and that of the New York Public Library.

pain, some graver sorrow, some grander woe, but all who spoke
momentarily bowed their heads only before raising them in lauda-
tory odes to the beloved dead. None doubted Emerson's greatness;
all saluted his public service. Why did they think him great? He
had achieved what no other American had even approached, a
literary and philosophical reputation esteemed in all parts of the
literate Western world. He had taught ideas and served ideals once
scorned but now championed. He had inhabited this world in
congenial comradeship with his fellow men. But he had dwelled
at the same time in a higher sphere of mind and heart which they
not only admired as the goal of life but themselves yearned for
only after life.

The *Boston Herald* tolled the news in mournful columns. "The
very worst fears have been realized. After a week and a day's
prostration, which threatened to end fatally from the beginning,
Ralph Waldo Emerson, poet, philosopher, and author passed
quietly away at 8:50 o'clock this evening. Thus another is added
to the long roll of geniuses, whose fame has been worldwide, and
who have gone so rapidly in succession over the dark river to join
the great and silent majority."[1] The *Boston Evening Transcript*
was too impatient on the occasion to wait for Emerson's actual
death to pay its tribute. While the sage of Concord still dozed on
his fevered bed, the *Transcript* called for "the most reverent and
affectionate expression of personal feeling." In awe and debt to
a beloved neighbor, the *Transcript* pondered the full meaning of
Emerson's life. "Emerson has been the teacher, the inspirer, almost the conscience of thousands of his countrymen." He has
stimulated thought as well as morality in convictions stated with
force and insight. "He had the strength and sweetness of the poetic
constitution, without any of its emotional vacillation. He shines
as steadily as the sun, and he never disappoints." Stimulating to

[1] *Boston Herald,* April 28, 1882.

the ablest minds, he has made the world "no less a debtor to his moral idealism." One could easily collect other evidence of "the moral heat that radiates from Emerson's work." Basking in that radiation, the *Transcript* soothed its grief with adoring gratitude. "He is like the sun not only in warmth and steadiness, but in attractive power; for it is impossible to turn his pages and not be drawn away from the excessive materialism in which we live to the finer atmosphere which he always breathed."[2]

This exultant elegy proclaimed many of the themes scattered by openmouthed mourners of Emerson, but the *Boston Daily Advertiser* mounted to even higher rhetorical idolatry. Here the deceased loomed as more than our greatest philosopher or profoundest thinker.[3] "He is a fresh, cool fountain from which one may draw indefinitely for the health and comfort of one's mind." No giant like Spinoza, not one of the "professed philosophers" like Fichte and Spencer, Emerson "did much better work, for he drew as it were the quintessence and very spirit out of God's world, and gave it freely, lavishly, exultingly to all comers." One finds "more in Emerson than truth, fancy, profundity, and daring courage; he has life, nature, mind, and correctly assumes that neither are our minds a measure of the world, nor have we begun to reach the whole of truth or the sum total of what is in nature, in life, and in ourselves." Such a potent guide to life quickly leads one to look for the source of his being. The search was short. Emerson is "the legitimate outcome of antecedent causes, of his environment, of his own will and work . . . hardly less the creator than the creature of his time, his country, and his birthplace, Boston."

[2] *Boston Evening Transcript,* April 27, 1882.

[3] It is interesting to note that this statement anticipates by two years the well-known dictum of Matthew Arnold which for a long time troubled American admirers of the great critic. Arnold's intention to emphasize Emerson's personal and inspirational qualities was lost sight of in the face of what seemed an unfriendly foreigner's debunking attitude. Yet the *Daily Advertiser* followed precisely the same line of reasoning.

By remaining apart from any school or set, he became "our common possession and our national glory, whose words read like the
great ledger entries of our merchants, whose acts betray the
shrewdness and prudence of the typical New Englander, and whose
words are the outcome of our national development—our joy, our
honor, and withal a part of every American. . . . If one wishes to
have the summary and quintessence of this new continent and its
people . . . it is all in Emerson, of whom only the mortal frame
can be destroyed by the angel death."[4]

In Boston, idol makers were skilled in turning images on the
wheels of hero worship, and this treatment of Emerson but began
a long labor of love. This study will watch their hands at work.
Yet geography had no control over the industry, and artisans elsewhere took up the task according to their lights. Without local
allegiance and less tied to the world, men, and events of Emerson's
career, the New York press could not generate such highly-charged
grief. Its editorial writers knew that he was a great writer, and
they saw a permanent place for him in American literature. The
New York Herald, for instance, respected Emerson as a stimulus
to "liberal thinking," and looked for the poetic qualities of his
writing, in prose no less than in verse, to "enroll" his work "among
classic literature." These are their enduring values rather than
"their pretensions to philosophy."[5] With greater emphasis, the
Times said "there can be no question that not only America's
greatest essayist is dead with him, but one of the greatest poets of
the English language." His eminence was temporarily clouded because "Emerson's writing is too supramundane, too much given
up to generalization, to make his readers feel the warm personal
affection that lesser men inspire." His enduring worth would yet
be recognized, however, for "if ever a man wrote for posterity,

[4] *Boston Daily Advertiser,* April 28, 1882.
[5] *New York Herald,* April 28, 1882.

it was Emerson, and though he be always a poet little read by the multitude, he will always remain a storehouse and a spring of suggestion and inspiration for poets to come."[6] The *Tribune,* on the other hand, emphasized the broader benefit of Emerson's work to the nation as a whole. "It is not the least of the services of Emerson and his school that they did so much to hasten the advance of the general esteem for the intellectual life which is one of the surest signs of national culture." Although Emerson's idealism seems hostile to modern science, Professor Tyndall, like hundreds more, hailed Emerson as the main impulse of his mind. "That his influence upon poets and scholars was incomparably more powerful than his direct effect upon the public is the true measure of his service to the intellectual development of his generation."[7]

In New York it remained for the *Sun* to show a powerful gratitude to Emerson, whom it called "a spirit of rare quality, whose powers have been devoted for half a century to large and lofty uses." Not the lute, not the pipe, but the harp was his instrument, "whose chords are strung in unison with the deepest and the highest emotions of the human mind." His verse challenges the instinct and lifts the spirit; his prose showers bursts of insight and uncovers primary facts. Though not a scholar or a systematic philosopher, Emerson has been a "generative" influence. "There are few aspects of human life . . . not the better known to us for his penetrating vision; and his writings are a storehouse of suggestion and admonition, a shining and enduring monument of genius and beauty."[8]

All this journalistic praise of Emerson, narrow and broad, careful or extravagant, showed surprisingly little grasp of Emersonian doctrine. Only the *Chicago Tribune* mirrored in its columns any

---

[6] *New York Times,* April 28, 1882.
[7] *New York Tribune,* April 28, 1882.
[8] *New York Sun,* April 28, 1882.

clear picture of the fundamental idea the deceased had served. Outspokenly the *Tribune* hailed Emerson as unequaled in human qualities. "How rare he was; how original in thought; how true in character. . . . Mediocrity comprehended him not." At the same time he was "inimitably" a poet, and "the spirit of poesy pervades his every thought." Introspective, an interpreter of human motives, an intellectual rather than a sentimental poet, he made not passion but mind "central" to his poems. He held "that the outward world is symbolical of the spirit expressed through it." Perceiving the scope of Emerson's thought, the *Tribune* showed how he gave flesh to his belief. Living an uneventful life, Emerson exceeded his physical sphere, although he perforce fulfilled the realities of life. His vision went beyond the world.

It was Emerson's belief that we create our own world by the purification of our own souls; that every spirit builds itself a house, and beyond its house a world, and beyond its world a heaven. In the world he saw a remote and inferior incarnation of God, and in every landscape a part of His face.[9]

Writers in the religious weeklies saw Emerson somewhat more narrowly. The liberal tended to extreme adoration. The editor of the *Index,* William J. Potter, glorified Emerson, who had been a founder and one of the twelve vice-presidents of the Free Religious Association, which published this weekly in Boston. Himself imbued with Emersonian values, Potter hailed the "rare moral nobility" of the man in whom heroic and saintly qualities were combined. Loving not only books but humanity and nature, Emerson exerted virtue, strength, and genius for the public weal, for human rights, for all classes and kinds of people. His books will last for ages to "feed the moral and spiritual hunger of mankind."[10] In effect, Potter was saying Emerson had fought for the ideals

[9] *Chicago Tribune,* April 30, 1882.
[10] *Index,* New Series, II (May 4, 1882), 518.

served by the *Index,* and in return his neighbors not only revered him but loved and understood him as well.[11]

A week later the *Index* printed in full a memorial discourse on Emerson delivered in Brooklyn two Sundays earlier by John Chadwick, who called himself a "Radical Unitarian."[12] With radical fervor the Reverend Mr. Chadwick saw Emerson's life an unstained portrayal of the perfect doctrines he preached. In *Nature* he early showed us "all things are moral," and throughout his long life, his acts spoke of his piety, his strength, his humanity. Idealist though he was, he always remained a realist whose practical sense kept him sympathetic to science. Thus he turned all knowledge and feeling, finally, toward the central principle, the Moral Law, truth, justice, righteousness. Having sanctified Emerson, the speaker turned to him for guidance as to a new body of scripture.

Plenty of honest judgments he will give us upon men and things. . . . Plenty of beauty . . . plenty of humor, too . . . and ever and anon, condensed into a startling flash. But over and above all this, it is the *spirit* of Emerson and the *influence* which proceeds from this which constitute his greatest value and significance for us. The love of truth, the love of beauty, the love of righteousness are not here or there upon his pages; they are everywhere. . . . If you are willing to let these deliver on your heart the force of their divine persuasion, you cannot go to him too often, for you will find it nowhere else more potently embodied than in the music of his words.[13]

[11] In the masthead of the *Index* (New Series, II *passim*) the Free Religious Association published its objectives: " 'To promote the practical interests of pure religion, to increase fellowship in the spirit, and to encourage the scientific spirit of man's religious nature and history'; in other words Righteousness, Brotherhood, and Truth. And it seeks these ends by the method of perfect Liberty of Thought. . . . It would thus seek to emancipate Religion from bondage to ecclesiastical dogmatism and sectarianism, in order that the practical power of religion may be put more effectively to the service of a higher morality and an improved social welfare."

[12] By this term Chadwick meant he rejected the miraculous and the divinity of Christ, preferring to see him as the world's most perfect man.

[13] John W. Chadwick, "Ralph Waldo Emerson," *Index,* New Series, II (May 11, 1882), 535–558.

The *Christian Register,* Boston's leading Unitarian weekly, matched this high-flown eulogy. In star and pebble alike Emerson saw the "gleam," and he "soared to heights of speculation." Though a mystic, he valued common sense and "never broke with the common mind." Though not a traditional poet, he cherished nature with a sensitive, profound sympathy, less an artist than "the friend and lover." A preacher who left the pulpit, "he never ceased to rebuke wrong, to expose shams, to uphold the good, to exhort the highest virtue. He could not get the preacher out of his blood."[14]

Those who spoke for other sects could not, however, give such free rein to their feelings. In Chicago, for example, the *Advance,* a Congregationalist weekly, acknowleged that Emerson had a strong influence on minds that needed him, but warned that others had been misled by his exaggeration and contradiction. Essentially a mystic and idealist with no system or logic, he revolted against forms and formalities, "obeying the strong impulse of his genius to express strongly the particular aspect of truth he so vividly sees." The editor did not question impulse or genius for Emerson, but others suffered because of his "failure to apprehend the Person and Mission of Christ." Urging men to value "the soul's direct intuition of the truth," he short-circuited the currents of dogma and institution, leaving the lights of faith unlit. Having shown the one flaw in the philosopher's stone, the *Advance* went on to burnish the glittering jewel with sweet sympathy.[15]

The *Christian Advocate,* a Methodist Episcopal weekly in New York, also made a gesture of difference with Emerson over doctrinal questions. Refusing to endorse entirely his religious utterances, it saluted him as a seer. He had learned "there is truth which transcends logic," and if he subsisted on his own intuitions, which gave him only "dim shapes of truth, still his effort was in

---

[14] "Ralph Waldo Emerson," *Christian Register,* May 4, 1882.
[15] "Ralph Waldo Emerson," *Advance,* May 4, 1882.

the right direction." Cool to the preacher, the *Advocate* embraced the man for his inspiring character.[16]

The *Churchman,* a New York weekly of Universalist belief, alone took a hostile stand against Emerson, denouncing his lattitudinarianism. Forced to confess that Emerson "will always have an honored place" as a thinker, this editor still fought his heresy. He substituted the personal consciousness of man for the Person of Christ; "his writings furnish little ground of hope that he had the Christian consciousness of the reality of the other world." Blind to Emerson's correspondential idea, to his sense of unity, the editor wagged his head. "Fine as Emerson's spirit is, and healthy as is his moral instinct, one is constantly reminded of what he fails to see. . . . Emerson's weakness in the spiritual realm is the weakness that comes out in the lives of all earnest men who seek to interpret life without the meaning thrown into it by the larger interpretations which the Church derives through Him who unites in Himself the instincts of men and the fullness of the Life Divine."[17]

In the eyes of literary commentators Emerson filled still another angle of vision. They gazed in awe and reverence at the literary man, who lived at breathtaking heights of nobility. In Philadelphia, for instance, the weekly *American* prophesied "the utmost that this generation can find to say of him will be thought by posterity not too strong for the truth." So graced was Emerson, said another writer for the same paper, that "no man lived more publicly than he; and yet few were more retired, having that power of withdrawing into himself, without asceticism or *hauteur,* which is the mark of high, serene contemplation."[18] The delicacy of this view contrasted with the historical mind of the *Philadelphia Daily Press,* which pointed to Emerson's greatness as a true Yankee, like Long-

[16] "Ralph Waldo Emerson," *Christian Advocate,* May 4, 1882.
[17] "Emerson's Ethical Position," *Churchman,* May 6, 1882.
[18] *American,* May 6, 1882.

fellow, of a breed now lost. In his life-span, the United States grew across a continent through the efforts of New England sons such as this one, whose indomitable spirit carried on the work of his indomitable forbears.[19] In *The Nation,* Thomas Wentworth Higginson saluted *Nature* and *The Dial* for the excitement they had brought a whole generation, for the challenge they had struck in a period of "conventionalism." Thus Emerson fostered self-reliance in literature. Yet Higginson found in his master more than doctrine. Rather than a philosopher he was a poet, of all "the most direct and unfaltering in his search for truth."[20] Beyond this he had another gift, "a nature so noble and so calm that he was never misled for one instant by temper, by antagonism, by controversy." Because the *Literary World* of Boston had commemorated Emerson with a special issue two years earlier, at his death it contented itself with a brief editorial comment. Now it measured Emerson for posterity. He "stands at the heart of things . . . less a reasoner than a seer, original in his thinking, independent in his judgment, sincere in his convictions." The author stressed the unity of Emerson. His "manhood matches his genius," his life was "the complement of his thought," and he "leaves a vacancy there is none to fill."[21] Writing for *Harper's,* Julian Hawthorne mingled the same helpless despair and joyous gratitude. "No one can ever take his place," he mourned, "but the memory of him and the purity and vitality of the thought and of the example with which he has enriched the world . . . will renew again and again . . . the summons to virtue and the faith in immortality which were the burden and glory of his song."[22]

As the presses rolled one voice strained to outstrip the other in praise for Emerson. The editor of the *Critic* spoke of the de-

[19] *Philadelphia Daily Press,* April 28, 1882.
[20] "Emerson," *The Nation,* XXXIV (May 4, 1882), 375–376.
[21] *Literary World,* XII (May 6, 1882), 144.
[22] Julian Hawthorne, "Ralph Waldo Emerson," *Harper's,* LXV (July 1882), 281.

ceased in proud, hushed tones as "the most elevating and purifying moral power . . . among the English races of the day." Even
more than a model for the Anglo-Saxon world, Emerson was the
ideal American, "the picture of a plain citizen, dear to his family,
useful to his neighbors, bound up in the affairs of a retired village,
worthy of the republican simplicity which De Tocqueville described thirty years ago." Yet the *Critic* preferred to think of Emerson as more than "a gracious influence in our national life." Essentially a poet, he dealt with virtue and beauty, order and law. "It
was this clean, pure atmosphere in which he lived, and the poetic
power, the high imagination, that helped him to marry mind to
the loveliest forms of matter."[23] In the same issue of the *Critic,*
two of Emerson's followers added personal outpourings of grief.
Whitman intoned a prose poem, "By Emerson's Grave," dwelling
on Emerson's heroism and crooning over his perfection. Perhaps
the life now ended, sobbed Whitman, "has its most illustrious halo,
not in its splendid intellectual or esthetic products, but in forming
. . . one out of the few . . . perfect and flawless excuses for being
of the entire literary class." Unstrung by the news, John Burroughs cried "With Emerson dead, it seems folly to be alive." A
darling of the gods now gathered to them, Emerson graced his
fellow-men with a rare privilege by living on the same earth with
them. "He scaled the empyrean in the guise of a quick and canny
New England farmer," yet through his pure, penetrating, far-
reaching genius, he incited men to "all noble thinking and noble
living."[24]

Vocal and solemn though they were, the original mourners of
Emerson sang but a prelude to the oratorio still to be composed

[23] "Emerson," *Critic,* II (May 6, 1882), 128. This editorial was marked
off with a heavy black border.
[24] Walt Whitman, "By Emerson's Grave" and John Burroughs, "Emerson's Burial," *Critic,* II, 123.

for his name. In the months after his death, as the grass grew over his grave, Emerson's followers covered his memory with garlands of lush praise. E. P. Whipple, a revered critic, planted in *The North American Review* an essay on "Emerson as a Poet." Whipple could not confine himself, however, to Emerson's poetry because of his moving spirituality. "He affirmed the supremacy of spiritual laws because he spoke from a height of spiritual experience to which he had mounted by the steps of spiritual growth." In his poems Whipple heard the voice of a man "whose character is as brave as it is sweet, as strong as it is beautiful, as firm and resolute in will as it is keen and delicate in insight—one who has earned the right to authoritatively announce . . . great spiritual facts and principles, because his soul has come into direct contact with them."[25] In effect, Whipple rejoiced that Emerson was a poet far more than he took delight in his poems. No matter one's purpose, one could exult in Emerson as poet. William T. Harris explained to readers of the *Atlantic Monthly* Emerson the "poet-seer" who had "the vision of the revelation of the mind in nature." As a seer, Emerson was the "law-giver" who proclaimed the true ethics of his generation, but he was also a philosopher because he set up one principle, the Over-Soul, as the explanation of all things. Harris singled out "The Sphinx" to show how Emerson caught the essential truth that "all nature and all history tell the story of the incarnation of the divine."[26] E. C. Stedman labored still harder to test Emerson's poetry for timelessness. In his verse, as in all his writing, said Stedman, Emerson set forth his spiritual philosophy, "holding always the idea of soul, central and pervading, of which Nature's forms are but the created symbols." For him art simply united nature with man's will, and thought symbolized itself

[25] E. P. Whipple, "Emerson as a Poet," *The North American Review,* CXXV (July 1882), 25.
[26] William T. Harris, "Ralph Waldo Emerson," *Atlantic Monthly,* L (August 1882), 242–246.

through nature's aid. "Thought, sheer ideality, was his sovereign; he was utterly trustful of its guidance." Such a pure mingling of thought, nature, and soul meant for Stedman the loveliest tones audible to the human ear. Emerson's poetic instinct inevitably led to the ideal image of poetry and Stedman drew from his verse time and again both the exalted spirit of the man and the eternal comfort of beauty.[27]

The grand, towering, but insubstantial image Emerson had become in the shade of death was most candidly unveiled by his former protégé, William Henry Channing, when he wrote to the editor of the *Modern Review* in London, apologizing for his failure to send an article on "the revered Emerson." Ill and unable to seize his opportunity, Channing praised the loving commentaries which had already "caught characteristic splendor from his glowing beauty, translucent truthfulness, human magnanimity, and symmetric manhood." Channing had hoped to crown these photographs by drawing from his own memory "two finished pictures of The Poet-Seer and Mystic-Saint." Predicting yet grander recognition for Emerson, he listed the blessings bestowed by this "peerless" man. "Merely by living," Channing testified, "he opened new possibilities of personal being, of human society, of heavenly communion, of immortality begun on earth. For his daily existence was so pure, ample, free, blissful, Eden-like, that the long-transmitted 'Curse' seemed transformed into the 'Beatific Vision.' "[28]

Emerson had not grown altogether unworldly for all his disciples, but even one who had sketched his likeness with a cautious hand soon trod the borders of idolatry. Once the good-humored cartoonist of Emerson "the transparent eyeball," Christopher Cranch turned to prose to draw a loving picture of Emerson the ethical and spiritual guide. Early in his career Emerson stirred

[27] E. C. Stedman, "Emerson," *Century,* XXV (April 1883), 886.
[28] William Henry Channing, "R. W. Emerson," *Modern Review,* III (October 1882), 850–854.

only the young, who read *Nature* as "a breath of morning and a vision of sunrise." Loyal to his convictions, nonetheless, he eventually led the way "into a life of thought, faith, and conduct [for] many cultivated men and women, who hardly know how much they have owed to this once almost isolated thinker." In Emerson's grasp of the "intimate correspondence of the outward to the inward, of nature to the soul," Cranch found the force of his doctrine. He is a seer, showing men not new truths, but old ones in a new light, the light of common sense and originality, not of tradition and dogma. Nearly half a century after they were first pronounced, Cranch applied Emerson's ideas to the needs of American life. His doctrine of self-reliance obeys divine law. "His lessons always point to the highest ideal of life. Every thought is the thought of a sage to whom truth is utterly empty and vain, if not moral and spiritual." Like his contemporaries, Cranch came at last to the judgment that because of his thought and feeling Emerson is primarily a poet. Many poems are faulty and uneven, he admitted, and his essays often lack continuity. These flaws arise from Emerson's way of seeing the meaning in things. Sharply he grasps a main idea, then buttresses it as he sees its needs. Yet often his poems sparkle, giving terse but noble expression to a lovely idea. His are always beautiful thoughts, intuitions of universal truths.[29]

Such a carefully drawn memorial was the prelude to the inevitable biography, which soon came from one of Emerson's lifelong associates, Oliver Wendell Holmes.[30] *Ralph Waldo Emerson* took a

[29] Christopher P. Cranch, "Ralph Waldo Emerson," *Unitarian Review*, XX (July 1883), 1–19.

[30] In the years immediately before and after his death, the memorial literature on Emerson included the following books: Moncure Conway, *Emerson at Home and Abroad* (Boston, 1882); George Willis Cooke, *Ralph Waldo Emerson: His Life, Writings and Philosophy* (Boston, 1881); Alfred Hudson Guernsey, *Ralph Waldo Emerson: Philosopher and Poet* (New York, 1881); Alexander Ireland, *Ralph Waldo Emerson: His Life, Genius, and Writings. A Biographical Sketch* (London, 1882).

genial view of a man Holmes admired for his excellent common sense and blameless character. Awake to Emerson's less desirable traits, especially what he thought transcendental mistiness, Holmes assessed Emerson with great frankness as a man, a teacher, a thinker, and a writer. He judged at the end that "by his life Emerson comes very near our best ideal of humanity."[31] Since this ideal image had grown from the author's long intimacy with his subject, the book held a peculiar local flavor. When George Bancroft discussed it in *The North American Review,* he simply dealt with old friends. He lauded Emerson's principles, his constancy, his tranquillity, his optimism, his faith in nature. These brought him celebrity and worldwide esteem. Now, beamed Bancroft, "to complete the measure of his happiness, Oliver Wendell Holmes, a favorite with the cultivated English-speaking peoples of two hemispheres, has risen up to be his biographer, and finds that he had no office but to relate how perfect Ralph Waldo Emerson was in sincerity, in the love of justice, and in devotedness to truth, to the beautiful, and to the good."[32]

With reason to be proud, as a Boston intellectual, of both Emer-

---

[31] Oliver Wendell Holmes, *Ralph Waldo Emerson* (Boston, 1885), p. 420. In sharp contrast is Holmes's memorial to Emerson at a regular monthly meeting of the Massachusetts Historical Society where tributes to the deceased member were the order of business. While other speakers praised Emerson in down-to-earth language, Holmes digressed at one point, endowing him with unearthly traits and making him the inhabitant of two separate worlds. "He dealt with life, and life with him was not merely this particular and air-breathing phase of being, but the spiritual existence which included it like a parenthesis between two infinities. He wanted his daily oxygen like his neighbors, and was as thoroughly human as the plain people . . . who had successively owned the house-lot on which he planted his hearthstone. But he was at home no less in the interstellar spaces outside of all the atmospheres. . . . It always seemed as if he looked at this earth very much as a visitor from another planet would look upon it. He was interested, and to some extent curious about it, but it was not the first spheroid he had been acquainted with. . . ." Massachusetts Historical Society, *Tributes to Longfellow and Emerson* (Boston, 1882), pp. 45–46.

[32] George Bancroft, "Holmes's Life of Emerson," *The North American Review,* CXL (February 1885), 142–143.

son and his biographer, Bancroft could scarcely hold any other image of the Concord sage. Other reviewers beyond the Hub shared his enthusiasm; and in regard to Cabot's *Memoir of Emerson,* based two years later on the same personal relation between author and subject, they applauded the same local ties binding Emerson to a lofty pedestal. As Emerson's chosen literary executor, Cabot had worked with zeal and care to gather the literary remains into as decent a state as he could for posterity. He won the gratitude of reviewers and editors everywhere. *The Nation* typically praised him for reviving Emerson's "largeness of mind, the persistence of his aims, his secure and absolute faith in the highest doctrine that he inculcates."[33] The *Atlantic* thanked Cabot for bringing Emerson "more distinctly into the light" as, with local pride, its reviewer concentrated on the emergence of Emerson's character through his break with Unitarianism and the ministry. Stressing his self-reliance, his loyalty to the higher law of his being, this writer showed Emerson growing out of the confluent circumstances of his background, his personality, his era. One may take great interest, he decided, in the facts about Emerson's home, habits, feelings, travel, friends, but the "weightier worth [lies] in the revelation which is afforded of the man himself in his self-discovery, in his expansion of nature, his growth of consciousness, in the very heart and secret of his genius."[34]

Whether for purity, nobility, inspiration, or self-reliance, Emerson was praised in continually mounting crescendo for two decades. Even before he died, admirers had spoken of him with awe and reverence. As his death receded into the past, they continued their monologues with much the same language but with greater intensity as he climbed farther and farther beyond earth-bound reach. Writing of "Emerson the Man" for the commemorative

[33] "Cabot's Emerson," *The Nation,* XLV (September 15, 1887), 216.
[34] "Emerson's Genius," *Atlantic Monthly,* LX (October 1887), 571–572.

issue of the *Literary World* in 1880, C. A. Bartol had called him a saint, "genial and pure." In 1889 William Thorne, a self-pro-claimed freethinker, called him "a beautiful soul." Reviewing the Cabot work, *The Nation* spoke of his "aspiring soul." A reviewer in *The Dial* praised the *Memoir* because it clarified the image many held of Emerson, which had become "extremely vague, and in some cases distorted"; yet he, too, sounded the familiar refrain, "In purity of life, and profundity of thought, he immeas-urably surpassed the majority of men."[35] As language for funeral sermons and published eulogies, such utterances were inevitable, and memorial incidents like the publication of biographies again brought them forth. Yet they filled as well a continual stream of articles strewn through the magazine press by elevated enthusiasts who seemed to draw vital breath from memories of their days in the heavenly sphere of the Concord sage. These testimonials reached their highest point in 1903 in the centennial of Emerson's birth.

For the central observance of this event, the Free Religious Association organized the Emerson Memorial School. George Willis Cooke described its plans in the *New England Magazine*. Two sessions of meetings would take place from July thirteenth to thirty-first, one in Concord's First Parish Church, the other in a Boston church. The foremost lecturers would speak on different aspects of Emerson's life and work. Elsewhere there would be services and lectures; and a memorial edition of Emerson's works edited by his son would help mark the occasion. Rev. Mr. Cooke spoke of the spontaneous, enthusiastic movement to honor Emer-son in the hundredth year of his birth, which "justifies itself and

[35] C. A. Bartol, "Emerson the Man," *Literary World,* XI (May 22, 1880), 174; William Henry Thorne, *"Emerson and His Biographers," Globe,* I (October 1889), 55; "Cabot's Emerson," *loc. cit.;* Edward John-son, "A Memoir of Emerson," *The Dial,* VII, (October 1887), 116.

needs no elaborate interpretation." Those acting here honored the noble life of "a man of genius, a poet of high lyrical gifts, and a writer of pronounced individuality and consummate skill."

When he took up the usual refrain about Emerson, Cooke added a new theme, now essential to any discussion of him, democracy. Bluntly put, in Emerson "the spirit of democracy was incarnated," its love of liberty, its demand for personal freedom, its hope that all mankind should be uplifted and ennobled. Cooke listed Emerson's causes: the Indian, the Negro, women's rights, the common people, individualism. He was careful, at the same time, to show these principles were not primarily social or political but spiritual: "According to his view the vision of God may come to any man who desires it, and the deepest intuitions are for any who make room for them in the deeps of the soul." This doctrine it was that made Emerson a great democrat, "and taught him that all men are kin and have need for each other."[36] In praising Emerson the democrat, Cooke did not overlook the great ethical teacher who instills a desire for moral right. His simplicity, his trust in the soul, his direct intuition of spiritual reality Cooke called the religion of Emerson, "one of the perennial men." Contentedly Cooke counted the blessings in this man, the people's ageless possession. "Such was the breadth and compass of his mind he was of no party, no sect, but belonged to mankind. His common sense was of near kin to his intuitive power, and his gift was not less as an ethical teacher than as a seer. Such being the man, his fame grows, and is ever more firmly established. In him we see the truest American, the man most worthy to teach and inspire us."

When the Concord philosophers and the New England clerics breathed the heady air of Emerson's American religion, they swelled their chests in customary group calisthenics. Exercising themselves over his ideal character and doctrine, they simply

[36] George Willis Cooke, "The Emerson Centennial," *New England Magazine,* New Series, XXVIII (May 1903), 255.

strengthened old beliefs. Other men could see Emerson differently. For example, Charles William Eliot, the president of Harvard, spoke at the centennial celebration in Symphony Hall, Boston. A chemist first and an educator second, Eliot confessed that as a youth he had found Emerson meaningless. With a broader perspective and heavier responsibilities, he later found Emerson's independent thinking useful in practical affairs. To his audience Eliot spoke of Emerson as a seer whose vision pointed the way to solving modern problems in education, social organization, and religion. He argued from "the indisputable fact" that Emerson's thought had kept pace with the fruitful thinking and acting of two generations since his working time. To this practical importance Eliot added "the sweetness, fragrance, and loftiness of his spirit" to record for Emerson "an enduring power in the hearts and lives of spiritually minded men."[37] In the broader world of affairs, *The Nation* observed Emerson's centennial with an editorial concerned, it asserted, not with the things countless voices were noting, his power of rhetoric, his inspiration as a thinker, his achievement as a poet, but with a "humbler theme," Emerson the citizen. In his actions as well as his teachings he preserved an independent mind, guarded human freedom, and upheld the dignity of man. He spoke out for free speech, he defended the Indians from exploitation, he defied the Fugitive Slave Law, he defended John Brown. Thus *The Nation* saw in Emerson the patriotic citizen "who would not sit silent when base deeds were being done in the name of country." By contrast, educated men in his time and ours show "fastidious indifferentism," and Emerson's example of civic duty "is no small part of his contribution to the strength and greatness of this nation."[38]

All the themes in Emerson, patriotic, human, and spiritual, were

[37] Charles William Eliot, "Emerson as Seer," *Atlantic Monthly,* XCI (June 1903), 855.
[38] "Emerson the Citizen," *The Nation,* LXXVI (May 28, 1903), 428–429.

combined in a fortissimo outburst in the *Outlook*. He early fought
a materialism which has since grown beyond what even he could
foresee. He pronounced the intellectual and spiritual emancipation
of the United States. He based his vision of independence and self-
reliance "on more massive foundations than political freedom . . .
on a fundamental conception of the immanence of God in the
world and the divinity of the human soul." He saw democracy
as faith in all men because there is something divine in all men;
and after accepting the fatherhood of God, he extended to all His
children the common principles of a self-governing family. When
Emerson answered Carlyle's challenge to explain the meaning of
America, he defined American idealism "more profoundly than its
greatest statesmen" by his belief in love and justice and brotherhood. Through his clear sight of everyday things he witnessed
"the reality of the Ideal." By Emerson "sent of God," the editor
is reminded that "the spiritual world is the only real world in the
sense that it is the only world in which men really live. . . ." Emerson preached faith, hope, and enthusiasm, a message of wisdom
for youth, a doctrine of "purity and the clean hand." His voice
today still urges the young to great deeds; and those who follow
Emerson will "make a new way for humanity . . . bring freshness
and health into the close air of the world . . . bring in the kingdom
of God."[39]

Having reached the realm of the spirit where the blessings of
democracy gained eternal strength, the shade of Emerson now
rose to the apogee of human aspiration. The piercing eye of the
literary critic alone could arch that heavenly distance. Hamilton
Wright Mabie commemorated Emerson's birth by appraising him
for twentieth-century America. Immediately he pointed to the
spiritual emancipation Emerson gave the new nation with "The
American Scholar." More than a blow to provincialism, this ad-

[39] "Ralph Waldo Emerson," *Outlook*, LXXIV (May 23, 1903), 210–213.

dress held in its theme of self-reliance the key to American life, to American character, to American destiny in the world at large. With no visible boundaries to his thought, Emerson united experience and faith, penetrated into "the spiritual realities behind the shifting appearance of the world," and valued the beauty of the human spirit. He attached a "supreme importance" to man as man which is the fundamental attitude of democracy, "not as a form of political or social order, but as . . . a recognition of man's spiritual significance, the consummation of the long process of history in the complete emancipation of the individual spirit, with full freedom to choose for itself its manner of life and the type of its development." Thus Emerson, "the incarnation of democracy," proclaims the manifest destiny of all mankind. He is allied "with the historic movement which came to clear consciousness in his work and which found its institutional expression, on a great scale, in the New World." At Stonehenge with Carlyle, when he unfolded his dream of universal love and brotherhood, Emerson became a prophet. He revealed America as a new human experience, "a spiritual conception of man as an original creative force; a recognition . . . of the divine in man which makes it safe to trust him. . . ." With fire in his eye Mabie assessed Emerson's life and thought as a national treasure.

He explained America to herself in terms of the spiritual life, he set man in his true place in the New World, he has kept the conscience of the nation and established for all time the doctrine that the success or failure of the new society shall be measured by its service to the emancipation of the soul, the exaltation of man.[40]

Like the grand panegyrics at the time of Emerson's death, these extravagant pronouncements on his centennial are not surprising in themselves. As a national possession Emerson could only excite

[40] Hamilton Wright Mabie, "Ralph Waldo Emerson in 1903," *Harper's,* CVI (May 1903), 903–908.

among high-minded admirers visions of an ideal attainment he himself had enjoyed in the buoyancy of his youthful hopes. Yet the shape and pose of the statue these consecrators erected clashed with the figure of the man and the spirit of his beliefs. What had happened to Emerson's modesty, humility, reasoned conviction, thoughtful individualism? Why this gloating self-righteousness, this insistent pride, this endless beseeching? Regarding the two decades between Emerson's death and his centennial, the historian can piece together an answer by seeing here at work the cult of the Genteel Tradition, which held literature and the arts in an unyielding grip of ethical principle. This was not the insistence upon passionless monogamy and Platonic love, as the Genteel Tradition has been mistakenly understood only recently,[41] but firmly bound, primly tied middle-class morality. It aped the social and intellectual fashions of Europe, especially of England, to which it looked with perplexed pride for its Anglo-Saxon heritage. At the same time it stood triumphantly upon American principle, the foundation of which was individualism. In the common man rested the power, the meaning, the hope of the future. To this doctrine of national pride, the Tradition allied the inherited beliefs of Christian idealism, which had sloughed off the forms of Puritan dogma and other institutional remains, grasping only the gossamer thread of a spiritual sanctity woven from the dreams of a lovely afterlife. Grounded in the Protestant ethic of individualism, work, righteousness, and leadership, this outlook held to a belief in self-help, cultural and moral as much as economic, which was the pillar sustaining the entire edifice.[42]

A striking illustration of how this cult worshipped its idols

[41] See William Wasserstrom, *Heiress of All the Ages* (Minneapolis, 1959).

[42] See Howard Mumford Jones, *Guide to American Literature and Its Backgrounds since 1890,* 2nd ed. (Cambridge, Mass., 1959), pp. 111–114, for an outline of this literary and artistic point of view, and for a list of literary documents which state it.

and dazzled its victims is found in *Counsel Upon the Reading of Books,* six lectures presented at Philadelphia to the American Society for the Extension of University Teaching, in the winter of 1898–1899. Delivered by esteemed authorities of the day, such as Brander Matthews on fiction and Agnes Repplier on memoirs and biography, these papers were prefaced by Henry Van Dyke who spelled out the doctrine of self-help for man's ultimate conquest of space and time. There are, he explained, three types of readers: the "simple reader," who reads for pleasure in his spare time; the "intelligent reader," who looks to books for information; and the "gentle reader," whom everyone should hope to be. He is "the person who wants to grow, and who turns to books as a means of purifying his tastes, deepening his feelings, broadening his sympathies, and enhancing his joy in life." Literature the gentle reader loves, Van Dyke continued, "because it is the most humane of the arts." Here he finds "expressions of the human striving towards clearness of thought, purity of emotion, and harmony of action with the ideal." Seeking "the culture of a finer, fuller manhood," the gentle reader turns to the books "in which the inner meanings of nature and life are translated into the language of distinction and charm, touched with the human personality of the author and embodied in forms of permanent interest and power. This," he concluded, "is Literature." Gazing thus onward and upward, the counselor placed the goal of life in books, not in life itself. Books become the means of human fulfillment, the field of ultimate triumph. For the gentle reader acts not from duty, fashion, or ambition, "but from a thirst of pleasure . . . a real joy in the perception of things, lucid, luminous, symmetrical, musical, sincere, passionate, and profound." Such pleasure restores the heart, "makes it stronger to endure the ills of life and more fertile in all good fruits of cheerfulness, courage, and love."[43]

---

[43] *Counsel Upon the Reading of Books* (Boston, 1900), pp. 14–17.

Behind this plea for the common man's culture there lay two important assumptions. First, the cultural leaders arrogated to themselves absolute authority in matters of art and intellect. Under shelter on one hand of Christianity and on the other of the universities, themselves largely the satrapy of Protestantism, they stood armed with sanctity, conviction, knowledge, and experience. The pervasive Christian morality which had always ruled American society gave the whip hand to moral sanctions. And the homogeneity of a supposed Anglo-Saxon heritage barred the restless radicalism invading much of American life. Second, the good books themselves were drawn not from the gentle reader's immediate culture but from the common inheritance of Western civilization. Homer, Vergil, Dante, Shakespeare, Milton were the great writers who would make "the eye clearer and the heart more sensitive to perceive the living spirit in good books." Composed and confident, Van Dyke advised the reader to be "serious, earnest, sincere, in your choice of books, and then put your trust in Providence and read with an easy mind."

The ascent of Ralph Waldo Emerson to the realm where the gods of culture reigned for the good of man's spirit completed the scheme of reverence dear to the Genteel Tradition. Said Bliss Carman in *The Poetry of Life,* in 1905, "The attempt which literature makes to deepen our feelings about a subject is the spiritual purpose of art." That purpose supports art in its duty "to make us happy, to give us encouragement and joy, to urge and support our spirits." After all, the possession of his immortal spirit is in itself man's supreme treasure, not only the ultimate source of joy but the primeval element of life. One day Emerson appeared, an "intrepid spirit" who freed men from the bondage of old dogma and revealed "the breath of goodness at the heart of things." What less could this man be than a prophet, a seer? What more could one ask from one's country, from literature, from democracy? From his generation, Carman said, Emerson won "a unique loyalty and enthusiasm, and we came to look upon him with that tender reverence which unquestioned goodness always inspires."

In the structure of Emerson's death one sees the genesis of a national achievement. Moved to articulate grief by the loss of a man they valued for his life, his example, and his message, his countrymen made of his death something new. They began by praising his merits. They soon glorified him. Then, time alone briefly stayed their hands before they raised him still higher, above the sphere of mortal man to where the handful of humanity's greatest donned the robes of immortality. At last an American mingled with the literary masters. At last America had its own apostle of light. On his death Emma Lazarus had wept over "one of those radiant lives scattered at wide intervals through history, which become the fixed stars of humanity." Half a century later, Van Wyck Brooks closed his biography of Emerson with a whispering passage that measured the orbit of this new star.

Gradually, year by year, the outline had grown indistinct, and the halo gayer and brighter, till at last there was left only a sense of presence. And the strong gods pined for his abode; for the universe had become his house in which to live.[44]

---

[44] Emma Lazarus, "Emerson's Personality," *Century,* XXIV (July 1882), 454; Van Wyck Brooks, *Life of Emerson* (New York, 1932), p. 351.

Selected Bibliography

The so-called *Complete Works* of Emerson as well as his *Journals* were edited more than fifty years ago in the fashion of the time. The *Journals* are now being re-edited with meticulous fullness and thoroughness by various scholars, with William Gilman as chief editor. To date six volumes of *The Journals and Miscellaneous Notebooks* have appeared, starting in 1960; sixteen are planned in all. A plan is under way to edit the complete works according to the same high standard. Two volumes of *The Early Lectures* have appeared, the first in 1959, edited by Stephen E. Whicher and Robert E. Spiller, and the second in 1964, edited by Whicher, Spiller, and Wallace E. Williams.

Ralph Leslie Rusk edited the six volumes of *The Letters of Ralph Waldo Emerson* (1939) and wrote the best biography we have, *The Life of Ralph Waldo Emerson* (1949). The most significant supplement to Rusk's *Letters* is probably *The Correspondence of Emerson and Carlyle* (1964), edited by Joseph Slater. The best critical study of Emerson's writing is Sherman Paul's *Emerson's Angle of Vision* (1952). It focuses on his principle of "correspondence." In *Freedom and Fate* (1953) Stephen Whicher has written what he has correctly called "an inner life" of Emerson, especially in his thirties. The most perceptive analysis of Emerson's mind and art as related to the transcendental movement is a classic of its kind, F. O. Matthiessen's *American Renaissance* (1941).

The amplest repository of material, of all sorts, relating to Emerson is without question the *Emerson Society Quarterly* (1955—   ), edited by Kenneth Cameron.

CARL BODE, born in the Midwest, received his degrees from the University of Chicago and Northwestern University. He teaches at the University of Maryland. He has been awarded Ford, Guggenheim, and Newberry fellowships, and is an honorary fellow of the Royal Society of Literature in the United Kingdom. His books include two in the field of American cultural history, as well as a collection of essays and two volumes of poetry. He is the editor of the *Collected Poems of Henry Thoreau,* co-editor of Thoreau's letters and of two volumes of selections from Thoreau's writings. Currently he is writing a biography of H. L. Mencken.

✪

AïDA DiPACE DONALD, General Editor of the American Profiles series, holds degrees from Barnard and Columbia, where she taught American history, and a doctorate from the University of Rochester. Mrs. Donald has been awarded A.A.U.W. and Fulbright fellowships and has edited *John F. Kennedy and the New Frontier.* She is also co-editor of the *Diary of Charles Francis Adams.*